Here's How

Start and Run a
Successful
Independent
Consulting
Business

Here's How

Start and Run a Successful Independent Consulting Business

DOUGLAS B. HOYT

NTC LEARNINGWORKS

NTC/Contemporary Publishing Company

Library of Congress Cataloging-in-Publication Data
is available from the United States Library of Congress.

Cover illustrations by Art Glazer

Published by NTC LearningWorks
An imprint of NTC/Contemporary Publishing Company
4255 West Touhy Avenue, Lincolnwood (Chicago), Illinois 60646-1975 U.S.A.
Copyright © 1997 by NTC/Contemporary Publishing Company
Printed in the United States of America
International Standard Book Number: 0-8442-2482-0
18 17 16 15 14 13 12 11 10 9 8 7 6 5 4 3 2 1

Contents

**How to Manage Your Back Office and
    Business Affairs   127**

Introduction

If you have decided to become an independent consultant, are weighing whether to do so, or are interested in strengthening and improving your independent consulting practice, this book will assist you.

Becoming a successful individual practitioner, contractor, or consultant interests a great many people, for a variety of good reasons. One is the desire to be independent, be an entrepreneur, run your own show, directly control your own destiny. A second reason is that consulting is becoming a more practical option; today's travel, communications, and computer facilities make it easier than ever before. Finally, corporate downsizing requires many to shift career directions, and many companies prefer hiring contractors instead of employees where possible, for cost control and added flexibility.

A March 1996 report in *The New York Times* on downsizing shows that well over three million jobs were eliminated each year from 1991 through 1995, about half of them white collar and managerial positions. Many of those in management and technical jobs have opted to sell their services on a contract basis as independent practitioners rather than to seek new positions as employees.

A survey for AT&T concluded that about 25 million Americans run business from their homes.

The bibliography of this book lists a great many current books on home-based businesses and related topics. There are many, many more. This book covers the essential aspects of how to begin and operate an independent consulting practice, the necessary personal requirements, the steps required to get the business underway, and, most important, the difficult and demanding methods for marketing what are often intangible services. To provide practical aid in starting and running the business, this book contains examples, forms, checklists, and exercises.

Another practical feature is Appendix A, which describes six successful individual consultants—what their specialties are, how they got started, how they market their services, and examples of the engagements they have done. These successful consultants explain their philosophies on how to run a business properly and make it successful. They are diverse individuals in a wide range of specialties, but each has initiated and operated a business and done well at it. You may wish to review Appendix A first, to get a picture of what independent consulting is all about.

A recent piece in *The New York Times* reviewed the diverse approaches of the many business success books. Some deal with "how to" techniques. Those are important. Others deal with attitude, which is also important. The author concluded that the best resource for developing a winning attitude was the children's book, *The Little Engine That Could*. The little engine's chant "I think I can, I think I can," is the classic demonstration of the attitude and spirit necessary to make any enterprise successful. This book explains both the action steps and the attitude you need to achieve independent consulting success.

Consulting Field Overview

1

Highlights of the Book

This book is arranged in loose chronological order, though all the parts are closely interrelated; marketing, which is discussed in the middle of the book, has to be done most of the time. But the book starts out by discussing what consulting is all about, what it takes to be a consultant and how being one affects your lifestyle. This first chapter may help if you are weighing whether or not to make a career in the consulting field.

The steps to get a consulting business underway are reviewed next, followed by how to perform consulting assignments as well as what many consultants also do, the giving of speeches and seminars, and the writing of articles, books, newsletters, and other material. Then, probably the most important part for most readers, are the ways for marketing consulting services.

Marketing is essential for independent entrepreneurs. Getting new engagements and clients is a necessary function for success, has to be done indirectly, for the most part, and is the major reason for failures when not done properly. Networking is a principal means of generating business, and participation in associations is one important way to network.

To stay on top technically and professionally, consultants must both be, and be regarded as, leading practitioners or experts in their specialties. Chapter 7 reviews the ways to achieve the necessary status in your field. Finally, maintaining your success is discussed in Chapter 8, which offers advice on how to manage your office, accounting, reports, billings, computers, and personal finances—including insurance and pension reserves.

Appendix A reviews the careers of six successful independent consultants, all widely different in their specialties, style, and personalities. But each one has a special way of becoming successful, and the appendix reviews their individual philosophies and career paths. It highlights their engagements, explains how they obtained and performed them, and describes the results they achieved for their clients.

What a Consultant Is and Does

A consultant is generally considered to be a guide and assistant to an organization or individual. Consultants have special knowledge and skills which they use to provide advice, solutions, or assistance to clients. Usually consultants, by definition, work on a contract basis, rather than as employees. This infers, too, that the service consultants give is of limited duration.

So these features of consulting—guidance, assistance, expertise, and temporary contract—describe the relationship between consultants and their clients. Consultants must continuously sell because each engagement has an end, and success depends upon securing future contracts and clients. Therefore, this book gives great emphasis to the merchandising of consulting services.

Consultants can perform most any activity. Typical services generally regarded as suitable for consulting are engineering, research, computer science, strategic planning, marketing, production, and materials handling. All of these activities can be, and are, done by employees. So it is not the function that makes it consulting; the relationship with the person or organization served defines consulting.

Actually, the consulting relationship is the same as that established by independent individuals performing other specialties—doctors, lawyers, plumbers. All of these may work on a contract or billing basis with their clients. The term could also include investment bankers who give top level guidance to major corporations on planning and implementing acquisitions, mergers, and divestments. While these professionals are not generally considered consultants, many of the marketing and business management principles in this book also apply to them.

This book does not explain how to be a good engineer, computer specialist, strategic planner, or whatever. It assumes that specialists who plan to be consultants have the required expertise in their field. What this book covers are activities that a person must perform as a consultant which are not required of employees. These consulting functions include making proposals, negotiating with potential clients, dealing with clients' personnel, making reports and presentations, and, most important, marketing to secure future engagements.

The recent downsizing in businesses and other organizations has resulted in an increase in independent consulting for two reasons. Many experienced and well-qualified people, especially among middle management, have been released and have found that selling their services on a consulting basis meets their career needs. Secondly, after downsizing, organizations find it economical and flexible to use consultants rather than employees to fill their fluctuating operating, technical, management, and operations needs.

History of Consulting

The field of consulting has been dominated by fairly large firms, although there have always been individual specialists performing consulting services independently. The Arthur D. Little Company, founded in 1886 in Cambridge, Massachusetts, was one of the earliest consulting organizations. It is still an industry leader and specializes in engineering related research.

A growth period for consulting began around World War I, initiated by the pioneering work of Frederick W. Taylor and Frank and Lillian Gilbreth. Their methods for improving worker productivity led to general use of time studies. Companies were eager to have outsiders help them install the new methodologies which enabled them to control costs better and often reduce them dramatically.

A small group of engineering organizations in 1929 formed a trade association they named the Association of Consulting Management Engineers (ACME). In the next couple of decades, leading ACME firms like Booz-Allen & Hamilton and McKinsey & Co. widened the range of their services to include strategic planning, policy, and finance matters. Consulting businesses grew in scope and diversity from World War II into the 1990s. New small firms were established, and older firms grew and sometimes merged with others to meet new business needs. Considerable growth occurred in human resources planning, and a burgeoning new area developed with the computer, which made for a large new segment of the consulting industry furnishing information systems design, advice, and support. During this period, public accounting firms found that they could readily help their audit clients solve computer, human relations, and all sorts of other problems; so most of them have established consulting branches which have become a strong force in the consulting industry today.

Groups of consultants in 1968 formed the Institute of Management Consultants (IMC), a professional association which certifies qualified members and otherwise acts to further the industry's and its members' interests. IMC and ACME established an umbrella organization, the Council of Consulting Organizations (CCO) in 1989. Also, an Independent Computer Consultants Association (ICCA) was formed in 1976 and now has over 1,700 members. In 1993, the consulting industry produced annual revenues of over $100 billion, according to U.S. Department of Commerce reports.

Structure of the Consulting Industry

The organizations above (IMC, ACME, CCO, ICCA) are voluntary groups of leading consultants and consulting firms who have established codes of ethics and otherwise try to maintain high standards of professionalism and performance. But they represent only a fraction of the total consulting businesses. No governmental certification or regulation exists for consulting, unlike accounting, law, medicine, and engineering. IMC has a certification program, based on tests, reviews, education, and demonstrated experience. But a few other organizations also have certification processes, each using different criteria.

So the consulting industry is unstructured. Anyone can claim to be a consultant and compete with others in the same specialty. And many are doing just that as the number of corporate positions dwindles. IBM reduced 100,000 jobs in six years; GE eliminated 100,000, cutting eleven management layers to four; and AT&T announced in January 1996 that 40,000 middle management cuts were coming soon. Many of these middle managers are turning to consulting. *Information Week* magazine reported that several former Chief Information Officers (CIOs) of major corporations have banded together to offer their advisory services to clients on a consulting basis.

Variety of Business and Technical Areas

Most management and technical functions can be performed on a contract basis by consultants rather than by employees. The 2,600-member Institute of Management Consultants (IMC) lists the specialties of its members within the following groups:

> Administrative Services
>
> Finance and Accounting
>
> General Management
>
> Government Administration
>
> Human Resources
>
> Information Technology and Systems
>
> International Operations
>
> Manufacturing Administration
>
> Marketing
>
> Materials Management
>
> Packaging
>
> Physical Distribution/Logistics
>
> Purchasing
>
> Research and Development

Each of these groups includes from 5 to 39 individual specialties. For example, Human Resources includes 38 specialties, such as Labor and Union Relations, Outplacement, Relocation Management, Time Management, and Wage and Salary Administration.

IMC members are also classified as to their involvement in the following industries:

> Agriculture, Forestry, and Fishing
>
> Construction
>
> Cross-Industry
>
> Finance, Insurance, and Real Estate
>
> Government
>
> Manufacturing
>
> Mining
>
> Nonclassifiable Establishment

Services

Transportation, Communication, Electric, Gas and Sanitary

Wholesale and Retail Trade

These industry groups are further broken down into up to 21 subclassifications.

These categories are representative of traditional management consulting. But, as we said, consultants can perform almost any function, in any industry. There are political consultants, bridal consultants, individual financial advisors, grooming and image consultants, home decoration consultants, and career counselors. Any special knowledge or ability that allows you to offer beneficial advice or service to another person or organization can be the basis of a consulting business.

Statistics Showing Growth

The latest five-year change data from the U.S. Department of Commerce show that total consulting revenue in 1992 was $72,610 million, up 86% from 1987, and the number of consulting employees was 674,411, up 33% from 1987. In 1994 total revenues jumped to $110,158 million. Further details are in the following table.

Consulting Revenues, Employees, and Establishments

Kind of Business	1992			1987	
	No. of Estab-lishments	Receipts–Millions	No. of Employees	Receipts–Millions	No. of Employees
Computer Programming Services	23,365	$23,548	242,707	$14,170	184,222
Computer Integrated Services	5,011	14,805	97,602	7,090	66,288
Computer Facilities Mgt. Services	675	2,577	23,356	1,198	18,528
Computer Consultants	7,186	4,478	46,509	No comparable data	
Management Consulting Services	33,762	22,629	211,781	13,287	186,224
Business Consulting Services	12,628	4,573	52,456	3,326	52,412
Totals	**82,527**	**$72,610**	**674,411**	**$39,071**	**507,674**

Source: *1992 Census of Service Industries*, U.S. Department of Commerce, Economics and Statistics Administration, Bureau of the Census.

This chart shows the size and trends in the consulting field, although it is not absolutely clear which kinds of business are consultancy. (For example, Computer Integrated Services includes sales of software and hardware as well as computer consulting. The "pure" consultant would consider it a conflict of interest to both give consulting advice and sell related products.)

The chart shows that during the 1987–1992 period, the number of consulting employees increased 33%, whereas the total dollar sales gained 86%. Computer-related consulting is 63% of dollar sales, a truly dominant part of the consulting industry. A recent article in *The New York Times* states that an incredible 10,000 consultants were engaged in helping people to install Lotus Notes.

The consulting business is made up of small organizational units: the average number of employees per "establishment" was 8.2 in 1992. (But establishment in these reports means a separate place of operations, so that a firm with ten offices would be ten establishments in these reports.)

Future Outlook The 87% and 33% respective increases in revenues and people are rates that should continue or increase, if the current conditions prevail. Computers and information systems are changing at an ever-increasing pace and becoming more intricate in spite of Bill Gates' efforts to keep things simple. These rapid changes and added complexities increase the need for outside help, guidance, and problem solving as businesses try to stay ahead technically in order to keep alive competitively. An August 1995 issue of *Information Week* forecast that the major accounting and consulting firm, KPMG Peat Marwick LLP, will be adding more than 1000 consulting positions in the coming year.

In the general business arena, several trends are underway which should make for additional opportunities for consultants. Mergers and acquisitions hit an all time high in 1995, and yet other moves to separate big companies into smaller units continue, as with RJR Nabisco, ITT, and AT&T. The mergers are particularly heavy among the rapidly changing medical businesses and pharmaceutical companies. Both actions, merging and separating, often are accompanied by downsizing or other employee separations.

An obvious group to benefit from downsizing are outplacement firms, one of the fastest growing fields these days. Companies planning employee layoffs often want the advice and assistance of outside consultants, to help them determine where best to make their cuts and how to operate with a leaner staff. Restructuring and reorganization involves emotions, and outsiders can often assist management in making the objective, careful analyses necessary to ensure reasoned and fair decisions. Human relations advisors can help clients plan major moves so that the employees left behind are not embittered but maintain requisite morale.

Finally, after cuts are made and the staff is at its thinnest levels, peak loads and unexpected problems can be resolved by using outside consultants who are happy to provide service on a temporary basis. Change is the order of the day, and many consultants regard one of their chief talents to be acting as a catalyst, to help make things happen when management may be reluctant or hesitant to move ahead quickly enough.

Reasons Consultants Are Needed

Varied Types of Client Needs

Clients seek out consultants for a variety of reasons, usually some combination of the factors listed below, and sometimes all of them.

Unique knowledge or experience. A company which has developed a new consumer product and has no experience selling such a product may retain a marketing consultant to help design a marketing program and approach. A finance executive who has inherited an information systems function, but who has no experience with systems, may hire a consultant to appraise the new function, its strengths and weaknesses, and recommend actions to make it more effective. Or a consumer may ask an engineer to evaluate the soundness of a proposed home purchase. In these situations, it makes sense to take advantage of an outsider's particular knowledge and skills.

Trusted independent judgment. Top executives may have differences of opinion on an important decision. Someone whom they all respect and trust may be retained to study the issue and render an independent recommendation on which way to go. This can be something like securing an arbitrator or mediator. In such cases consultants offer a valuable new perspective on the matters in question.

Need for a catalyst, to get action. Perhaps an organization's leaders recognize their own failings in procrastinating, or really just don't have time to do things they know are important. A consultant in such a situation may be able to come in temporarily and get a job done by prodding those involved, or by coordinating the work of various people who must do different parts of a project. Such a consultant becomes an expeditor, coordinator, and facilitator, and contributor to the project.

Research. An organization may be weighing the pros and cons of venturing into a new market. But it does not have the staff to perform extensive research into all the factors involved: potential customers, manufacturing and distribution methods and costs, current and potential competitors' products. So the organization may fill its analysis needs best by hiring a consultant to do the job.

Temporary staff need. An information systems department may need to design and launch a new program quickly. To get the job done on time, it may retain a consulting organization to do the necessary systems and programming work, to document the system and train users, then leave. Most corporations prefer this solution to the alternative of hiring staff needed for the new program then releasing them when it is done, or trying to then fit them into the organization in other positions where they might not really be necessary.

To meet a time deadline. A company decides to decentralize its worldwide organization by a certain date, and realizes that it must redesign the accounting system to fit the new organizational structure. Working out the details will take much analytical time and coordination among executives concerned. The company decides to retain a financial consultant to meet their deadline and system goals.

To help reorganize, downsize, cut costs. Making drastic changes to organization relationships and severing employees involves a lot of emotions which can stand in the way of clear thinking. The experience of consultants who have done these things before and have an outsider's objectivity can be an important aid in properly planning and effecting such changes.

Different Types of Consultants

Different types of consultants best fulfill the various types of client needs outlined above. An article in the September 1995 issue of *AS/400 Systems Management* (published by Adams/Hunter Publishing) explained five different styles of consultants, as follows:

- *Brains.* High-level strategy consultants.
- *Gray Hairs.* Technical or industry specialists.
- *Methods.* Experts at applying proven methodologies and the project management techniques that go with them.
- *Products.* Vendors that provide software and/or hardware whose consulting focus is their proper implementation.

• *Implementation*. Consultants that produce a specific product under the direction of management.

Another way of categorizing the different consulting approaches and styles is as follows:

• *Generalists*. Consultants with wide experience respected for their good judgment who help clients define their problems and plan broad strategies, policies, and organizational relationships.

• *Specialists*. Consultants with considerable depth of academic training or practical experience in a relatively narrow field, such as an employee benefits specialist, a computer data base specialist, or a research chemist.

• *Experts*. Specialists whose reputations have achieved a high level of respect among peers, considered leading authorities in a particular specialty.

These classifications help convey the diverse types of services that consultants provide. If you are planning to enter the consulting field or are already in it, analyze your particular role and structure your marketing and performance approaches to fit that classification style. It is important to recognize that no one of these categories is more or less worthy than another. Each one has an important function to play in meeting the diverse needs of clients.

Exercise: Self-Appraisal as to Consulting Type

As a basis for self-evaluation, classify your type of consulting in the categories previously explained.

Consulting Type	Yes	No
Brains		
Gray Hairs		
Methods		
Products		
Implementation		
Generalist		
Specialist		
Expert		

What It Takes to Be an Independent Consultant

Independent consultants sell their knowledge, talents, and reliability. But all that can be summarized as reputation. If you have all of those requirements and are well known and famous, you may not have to seek out clients and further engagements; you may be selective in accepting work from clients who seek you out. But most independent consultants who have the requisite knowledge, talents, and reliability must continuously merchandise their services in a variety of ways that are discussed in some great detail later on. Successful independent consultants must have more than the ability to do a good job; they also must have the personal qualities to merchandise that ability and the talent for and interest in running their consulting business.

Knowledge and Skills

What every consultant who is successful has and sells is the ability to do a job a client wants done, and to do it well and professionally. The specialty may be the know-how to design a warehouse, to guide a politician's campaign, or to train customer service representatives. Whatever the nature of your skills, you must have experience and talent to do what the client wants done and to do it well.

You may have developed your skills and knowledge in school or on the job as an employee or as a consultant. Whatever the speciality, you have to be able to provide a service for a client that the client appreciates and values as well worth the cost.

Personal Qualities

A consultant's personal qualities and attitude are as important to success as is the technical ability to do the job at hand. You must have a somewhat adventuresome spirit, a desire to be an entrepreneur and to be your own boss, a willingness to accept risk, an ability to generate trust, and, above all, a determination to make your enterprise work. Each one of these qualities is essential to success.

Ability to generate trust. In all consulting relationships, clients put themselves on the line. Those who retain you have their reputations at stake; their peers will evaluate them based on the results of the job you do as consultant.

Therefore, clients are reluctant to proceed unless and until they trust you. Clients must feel confident that you will do a professional and effective job they, and their associates, will be proud of. This faith and trust are usually achieved over a period of time, possibly after several meetings at which you and the client get well acquainted. Such trust may already exist if the client knew you earlier in some business or social organization. It may be created or reinforced by a mutual acquaintance recommending your work. It may also be enhanced by credentials, a Ph.D., a book written, or prior clients who vouch for you. But however you create it, trust is a personal feeling, usually developed over time, a "chemistry" between two people.

Part of the trust a client has in a consultant is based on the consultant's attitude and manner. Such things as eye contact can indicate a sense of self-confidence. But confidence can be overblown; the crass huckster type usually creates suspicion and discomfort rather than trust. The laid back self-assured attitude is most often the style that fosters that all-important sense of trust for a consultant.

Trust is an essential ingredient of all sound consulting relationships. Undoubtedly the best way to develop trust is to perform an outstanding job for each client, who will then have the required trust that may foster further work through repeat assignments or referrals to others (though clients are reluctant to refer consultants to their competitors).

Determination and persistence. For the individual consultant there is no boss setting goals and following up for performance. No one else is setting the daily time schedule. As a consultant you must have a high degree of drive and determination to make things happen. In most small consulting businesses, there are slow periods, sometimes wide gaps between engagements. Those are the times to get out and work hard at the many, mostly indirect, ways to market the business's services. When obstacles arise, and they do, you have to figure out ways around them, and maybe start moving in another direction. This sense of drive and stick-to-it-iveness is another essential ingredient for successful individual consulting.

Entrepreneurial spirit. The entrepreneurial spirit is akin to determination and persistence. Entrepreneurial spirit is an enjoyment of adventure, a willingness for and excitement in taking risks, the pleasure of anticipating accomplishments and making progress toward emotionally charged goals. The future success of any business depends on the planning and perseverance of the leader, and he or she must accept that role and find satisfaction in taking full responsibility for the enterprise and its results. At the same time the entrepreneur must be flexible, take on opportunities as they present themselves, and be willing to change course when conditions indicate it is wise to do so. In short, the entrepreneur must be comfortable without a regular paycheck from an employer, or a 9 to 5 schedule. Most, in fact, will spend many more than the normal 35 to 40 hours a week, and will feel happy doing so because the work involves moving closer to achieving one's personal goals.

Merchandising Talent

The merchandising approach for individual consulting is quite different from that for commodities and other services. It takes time because it is mostly the planting of seeds that take some interval to develop. That means that consultants usually must develop a reputation, have their talents and skills become known through meeting people at business gatherings, show leadership in professional associations, if possible speak before groups, and write articles about their accomplishments and ideas. All those activities spread the word about their abilities and availability. These merchandising concepts will be explained in detail later on, but they are mentioned here to show the type of talent consulting requires. These activities require being comfortable with being gregarious. A few college professors and others may be sought out because of their reputations and may not have to consciously promote their talents, but most individual consultants do have to circulate and be active in professional and trade groups.

Some independent consultants do get some or all of their jobs through brokers, who secure the clients and take their brokerage fees. And there are also membership groups which provide their members with engagement leads.

Business Management Ability

As an individual consultant, you are running a business, whether you like it or not, and you should feel comfortable doing so. This means doing your own accounting, or hiring someone to do it, deciding on and arranging for a corporate or other business structure, and probably getting and operating a computer, faxes, copiers. It means following up for payment from clients. The individual consultant also should arrange for business and personal insurance and health coverage, and establish financial plans for retirement.

The individual consultant usually has to make written proposals and reports to clients, and possibly prepare presentation materials. As is often the case, consultants

secure others to share the work, which involves oral or written agreements and dividing the financial results. Lawyers are often needed to guide the making of agreements with clients and subcontractors.

All of these activities require time to perform, or to arrange for and supervise. These hours, which must be planned and allowed for, in addition to the merchandising time, are nonbillable hours; they are one reason individual consultants often work more than 40 hours a week. Part of the business skill consultants need is the ability to plan their finances so that their business and personal lives survive the valleys of the usually peak-and-valley cycle of consulting businesses.

Knowledge and Skills Worksheet

The following worksheet is designed to help you review your knowledge and skills as they relate to individual consulting success.

AREAS OF KNOWLEDGE AND SKILLS   ACCOMPLISHMENTS

List the five skills or areas of knowledge in which you do, or plan to, perform consulting services:	List here major accomplishments or other credentials which demonstrate capability in this field:
1	1
2	2
3	3
4	4
5	5

Exercise: Marketing Potential

For each of the five skills or areas of knowledge you listed in the previous worksheet, indicate the names of individuals or organizations who might be potential clients, or of the types of clients you plan to seek.

Knowledge and Skills	Client Sources
1	
2	
3	
4	
5	

Personal Qualities Worksheet

The following worksheet is designed to help you assess your personal qualities as they relate to the probable success of an individual consulting business.

Personal Quality	Fine	Good	Medium	Fair	Poor	Comments
Ability to generate trust and confidence						
Determination and persistence						
Entrepreneurial spirit						
Willingness to accept risk						

Merchandising and Business Worksheet

The following worksheet is designed to evaluate your readiness to tackle the merchandising and business management activities involved in running an independent consulting business. The answers are often not a clear-cut "yes" or "no." But the comments space is designed for brainstorming in areas where your answer is less than an enthusiastic "yes." You may use the comments space to note how you plan to improve that activity or get assistance in order to support your business plan better.

Question	Yes	No	Comment
Do you enjoy joining business and social groups?			
Do you enjoy speaking in front of audiences?			
Do you volunteer for committee and other tasks?			
Have you written articles for publication?			
Do you like preparing or analyzing financial reports?			
Are you comfortable doing word processing?			
Are you comfortable working spreadsheets?			
Are you comfortable using databases?			
Do you have adequate plans for insurance and pension?			

Rewards, Risks, Lifestyle

The lives of independent consultants differ from each other because consultants are individuals who enjoy and promote their special and unique qualities, each attempting in one way or another to stand out from the others. A few are prima donnas. And yet, with all their individual distinctiveness, they share in common certain rewards, risks, and lifestyles.

Rewards

The rewards for consulting are basically twofold: financial and personal satisfaction.

The financial rewards can be handsome. Some leading consultants can command a price of $10,000 or more for a speech or presentation. But most consultants are happy with a net take-home pay of somewhat more than what they might earn as an executive or employee performing tasks at a similar level of responsibility. To do that the consultant must have a billing rate of double the take-home pay of an employee, the second half to pay for the overhead such as office equipment, the job's fringe benefits such as medical and other insurance, pension provisions, and the time that must be spent marketing and managing the business, all nonbillable hours.

While the money may be ample or substantial, the main benefit is the feeling of full control over your life with the resulting enhancement of self-esteem. There is a real satisfaction to setting a goal of accomplishment and then achieving it. As one consultant put it, there is a fine sense of freedom to be able to plan and control each day on your own, with no boss to set your goals and monitor your behavior, and no corporate policies to conform to. True, you may not secure every client you seek, and obstacles occur that no one can overcome except you. But there is gratification in the feeling of independence that is hard to duplicate or compare with other satisfactions.

And the sky is the limit as far as financial rewards are concerned. As a consultant's reputation increases, so can the billing rate. As demand for services grows, the consultant can get others to assist, either subcontractors or employees, and thus increase the business's size, revenues, and profits.

Risks

The other side of the coin is the underlying risk of an independent business, including consulting. Absent is any assurance of a regular paycheck or income. The gross and net income fluctuate inevitably. Gone is the built-in corporate benefits package including paid vacations and holidays, sick leave, pension set asides, structured savings plans such as the 401-K, and life and medical insurance. These employee benefits can generate a feeling of financial security. Of course, these days with the trend toward downsizing and loss of corporate loyalties, all those structured benefits can evaporate in a moment's notice, and often do.

Further, in starting up an independent practice, unless you begin with a client or two, you can face a long waiting period before you can send out substantial and regular invoices. Some new consultants have the nail-biting experience of watching their life's savings dwindling away. This period of struggle can be of some duration because of the lead time between marketing efforts and the engagements, billings, and collections they hopefully generate.

Lifestyle   The hours are different, the place of work is different, the relationships with business associates are different, and the family relationships may be different. In total, the life of an independent consultant can be quite dissimilar from that of an employee.

Consulting entrepreneurs usually have longer and much more flexible work schedules than employees. Because of their personal stake in the business, most independent consultants spend many more than the 35 to 40 working hours a week normal for employed persons. But their work schedule is flexible. Consultants can schedule time off for a golf game or family outing without interfering with their client schedule.

Business relationships differ because clients and consultants are equal, not superior and subordinate. The client wants something done, and you offer to do it; you make a deal, and get the job done. Hopefully the deal is one which is satisfying to the client and the consultant. The consultant and client are equals, both benefitting from the relationship and from the deals they work out together.

This is quite different from having a boss who tells you what must be done and then oversees your work. Of course it is not quite that simple. In most employee positions, you also deal with many peers on your own level and may have several subordinates. But in every employee position, the boss-employee relationship is key.

Some independent consultants miss the camaraderie of day-to-day dealing with others in the office. Many do spend much time alone in their office, on the phone with clients and potential clients, writing articles or memos, and attending to other administrative chores. These consultants can fill some of that need for being with others by participating in professional associations and business groups. Most consultants find this type of networking to be an important part of their marketing, keeping them in frequent contact with other business and technical people.

Family relations can be enhanced or impaired by a shift to consulting, depending on the attitude and behavior of those involved. Of the six successful independent consultants profiled in Appendix A, two have established offices outside their homes, and four have made business offices as parts of or adjacent to their homes. In one case, the spouse has been a longstanding co-partner in the business. A main problem with an office at home is that the other family members' activities can be distractions, sometimes reasons for procrastination, and those situations can lead to tension that can harm not only the job but the family relationships. But those distractions can usually be ameliorated by discussing the issues and setting up appropriate work schedules and rules. None of the six persons interviewed for Appendix A reported any significant problem in this regard. Three of them expressed a particular enjoyment at being able to live in and work out of their suburban and rural environments.

Another potential for family stress for an independent consultant is the irregularity of income and, indeed, its uncertainty from time to time. The secret to resolving this possible stress is to be conservative and disciplined in planning the business and family budgets. Those budgets should be based on typical minimum, rather than peak, income so that peak periods provide a reserve to tide over those valleys.

How to Plan and Start an Independent Business

The first chapter reviewed what it takes to be a successful independent consultant and the rewards, risks, and lifestyle you may expect as an independent consultant. It also contained several worksheets to help you think about whether and how to proceed with your consulting career.

This chapter can assist you in deciding whether to launch an independent consulting business. It reviews the many varied considerations in making such a decision, then analyzes the planning steps you should undertake before starting the business to make reasonably certain that your plan is workable. This chapter ends with a review of the initial steps to getting your business underway: setting up the office, deciding on a name, and deciding on a corporate or other business structure.

Making the Decision   Some successful consultants had a burning desire to become consultants early on, and thought through their preparation steps and strategies before initiating their consulting businesses. Some had little or no early interest in consulting, but were approached by one or more people to assist or advise them in their business affairs, and grew into a consulting business as such opportunities presented themselves. The beginnings for most independent consultants fall somewhere between these two extremes. The reasons for deciding to take the consulting route, and the ways of getting into it, vary greatly. Usually, the desire to be your own boss, to chart your own destiny, and to be an entrepreneur is a significant conscious or unconscious part of the motivation to set up an independent consulting business.

Ways to Begin

The ways to get started are as varied as the reasons for deciding to pursue consulting independently. Some of the better ways to get the business launched, reviewed next, are to do consulting work part-time before leaving a job, to first learn the ways of consulting by working for a consulting firm, to have one or two clients lined up before leaving a job, and to begin consulting as a second career.

As a Part-time Activity

One excellent way to begin a consulting career is by arranging for consulting work to be done on a part-time basis during the nonworking hours of a regular job. Consultants who choose this method have the advantage of developing client relationships and consulting experience before cutting off their regular paycheck. If the consulting can then be increased after you leave your regular job, you can make for a smooth transition into consulting without the difficulty of leaving the security of employment before you have arranged for consulting work.

Two obstacles may hamper this type of transition. First, it is not always possible or easy to do client work on weekends and in the evening. Second, some employers, if they are aware of extensive outside consulting being done during off hours, may feel their work is not getting the full attention it deserves. They may even resent that the skills developed on their payroll are being applied to others for a fee.

On the other hand, some employers accept the outside consulting being done by one of their employees, and may even view consulting as a broadening experience for the employee, or as an admirable sign of ambition.

Leave a Consulting Firm

Other things being equal, it is easier to sell yourself as a consultant if you have had experience as a consultant. Also, doing consulting work as a staff member of a consulting firm gives you experience in the conduct of consulting projects. This is particularly worthwhile if you leave your consulting firm employer on good terms, so that reference checks will be favorable.

A touchy part of this situation is dealing with the firm's clients who like your work and want to retain you after you leave. There are ethical questions as to the propriety of accepting assignments from clients of your former employer, and also the practical disadvantage that the former employer may be less likely to give positive references after losing clients to you. Some consulting firms have employment agreements that establish restrictions in these types of situations.

Have a First Client or Two

If you are contemplating leaving an employed position to start a consulting business, you may be able to use your business contacts to arrange for a first consulting engagement before leaving the security of being employed. This is seldom possible, but it is an approach you should consider and pursue if at all feasible. It eases the transition to getting an independent business underway.

Former Employer as First Client

Having the employer you leave become your first client is an arrangement that happens with considerable frequency. This can often be done whether your employment separation is your choice or the employer's.

If you are planning to leave to start your own business, before the time comes to tell your employer, give some thought to your employer's problems and to unfinished business that you might help with on a contract basis after you leave. Then, when you do advise your superiors of your intentions, you can suggest ways in which you could later be of benefit to them. If the response is favorable, you can negotiate the terms of helping to fulfill their needs on a consulting basis, when you discuss the other arrangements for your departure.

Securing your first consulting work from the employer you are leaving is a strong possibility. Your former employer knows you and your capabilities well, and so should not have to worry about your competence or reliability, a worry usually present when a firm engages an unknown outside consultant. Another advantage to your employer is that you would not have to spend time learning the background for the project, time that another outside consultant would spend and would charge for.

If your departure is at your employer's initiative, due to downsizing or for another reason, it still may be worth exploring obtaining a consulting assignment. In fact, two additional factors make consulting possible when the departure is your employer's decision. First, when down-sizing occurs, there are obvious disruptions and it may be difficult for important tasks to get done with the smaller staff; so the employer may welcome having such obstacles alleviated by having your help on a contract basis. Second, asking an employee to leave is always a difficult and some-times painful thing to do, and the employer may be happy to do something to lessen the guilt of having to create a difficult personal problem for a loyal long-term employee.

As a Second Career

Some people have initiated second careers as a consultant after reaching retirement, sometimes earlier, having achieved much experience and ability in their field. These people are motivated by a desire for the flexibility, freedom, and control inherent in a consulting business. They have gained reputations for expertise among their peers. And these executives or technicians know that the work they can do is often a salable commodity on a contract basis.

Because retired people usually have vested pension arrangements, they are not as hard pressed as younger persons contemplating the launching of a consulting career, who are often without significant financial resources and have families and children to care for.

While second-career consultants have several advan-tages over younger people starting consulting careers, many still do encounter marketing obstacles to securing a steady flow of assignments. Though they may readily get jobs from their first-career contacts and reputation, they may find it harder to aggressively do the groundwork to develop continuing client engagements. In such cases, con-sultant brokers can be helpful and membership organiza-tions can provide referrals.

In most second-career consulting situations, consul-tants perform the functions in which they are experienced and skilled, but working on a contract basis rather than as employees. However, it sometimes is feasible to trans-fer one's experience and skills to a new but related role; for example, a bank officer who has advised customers might set up a business as a financial counselor to indi-viduals, putting his first-career knowledge and abilities to work in a new way.

The American Association of Retired Persons (AARP) says that about 25 percent of retired persons do full-time or part-time work.

A Product of Downsizing

Much of what has been said about second-career consul-tants also applies to those starting a consulting career as a result of downsizing.

Downsizing forces a second career on many people. Those who lose jobs to downsizing have many other people competing with them for available jobs or consulting work. A serious problem, in addition to these supply-and-demand difficulties, is the loss of self-esteem, which can be devastating, and feelings of bitterness and resentment. Those feelings can undermine one's effectiveness in seeking a job or consulting work.

Feelings of anger and resentment must be overcome because they impair a person's ability to seek a new job or consulting work in a positive manner. Being "let go" used to be a stigma that affected a person's reputation; that is no longer true because it is common knowledge that an abundance of top notch, highly capable executives have lost jobs due to downsizing in recent years.

Downsizing typically hits middle-aged people in middle management. One frequent feature of downsizing is the reduction of levels of management in the organizational hierarchy. Sometimes, more than half of the levels of management in a given organization can be eliminated. The problem in job seeking is that, typically, any employers who may be hiring managers are usually looking for younger people they can bring along, not the middle-aged or older executives with extensive experience.

Consulting has some advantages over job seeking for people who are downsized. First, downsized companies sometimes have job freezes, and management may work around that obstacle by retaining consultants on a contract basis to handle the work load. Second, with some ingenuity, executives may use their talents in different ways—as with the bank officer cited earlier who found some friends and others who were willing to pay him an appropriate fee to secure his expertise and counselling on their personal finances.

Making a Plan

Most authorities recommend having a well thought out plan before you launch a new enterprise. Many chapters and books have been written on the subject of how to write a business plan. A carefully written plan is essential if you plan to seek a loan or stock investors because any investor would be foolish to furnish funds without one. If the planned business is to be run by more than one person, it is also an absolute must that you prepare a detailed plan to assure that all parties are in clear agreement about how the business is going to work and how the responsibilities are to be shared.

But no commercial investor is likely to supply funds to a consultant about to launch an independent enterprise without a history of successful client billings. And most independent consulting businesses start off with a sole owner and operator, so partnership arrangements do not then need to be defined.

However, although a detailed written plan may not be necessary, it is certainly a wise thing to do. Seventy percent of successful consulting businesses have had no such plan. But it can be a useful device for one purpose only: to make sure your plan is well thought through before you start to spend your time and money to get it underway. Writing is part of the thinking process. Putting together in words plans for the services to be provided, clients to be secured, markets to be reached, merchadising methods, office plans, legal structure, and financial projections, can help ensure that you have considered all aspects of a proposed business and that the pieces of the plan fit together logically.

The plan need not be typed or even neatly written, unless you want a friend or associate to review it, which can be a useful idea. The friend or associate may offer comments and suggestions and look for any gaps and inconsistencies in the plan.

So after reading this book and possibly other literature on the subject, a good first step, before you spend money and time, is to prepare a plan in some detail, set it aside for a few days, maybe have someone else comment on it, look at it again and make revisions the review indicates would be desirable. Then, if you are sure of the wisdom of proceeding, move ahead.

Another value of the written plan is as a document to review and revise periodically. Initial planned directions and results never occur exactly as you expect and, indeed, flexibility in taking advantage of opportunities as they present themselves is an important part of growing and moving ahead. Comparing plans to actual developments helps you periodically think through where you've been and how things stand, and then adjust future plans based on current circumstances and expectations.

The plan should probably cover these features: services and products sold, marketing approach and methods, potential clients, comparison with competitive services and products, reasons why your products and services are preferable to those of competitors, your qualifications and experiences, office equipment and location, legal structure, and financial projections based on the plan's features and assumptions.

The following is a suggested outline for a consulting business plan, listing the topics and questions such a plan might well cover.

Consulting Business Plan Outline

Summary

This part should be written last, highlighting the important features of the plan. It should be limited to one page, a discipline which forces the writer to identify the most important points, such as: main service, why it should sell, competitors, expected profit (or loss) first year, and five-year growth expectations.

Services and Products

What is the main service to be offered to clients?

 Nature of specialty, e.g., engineering, finance, marketing.

 Kind of service, e.g., problem solving, planning, training.

What other advisory services may be made available to clients?

What other products or services may be developed and sold?

 Seminars?

 Writing of articles and books?

 Newsletters?

Explain competitive services/products for each of the above.

Describe features planned to be superior to those of competitors.

Marketing Strategies

Who are principal potential clients for services and products?

List contacts and potential contacts among potential clients.

How will potential clients learn of services and products?

Will you use brochure or flyers? If yes, sketch an outline of one.

Pricing

List planned price for each planned service and product.

List competitors' prices for related services and products.

Your Qualifications and Experiences

List pertinent education steps.

List pertinent employment positions.

List all pertinent accomplishments, especially measurable ones, e.g., sales increased, costs reduced, lead time cut. (These are key, and should become major features of marketing program.)

Office Location and Equipment

Office at home, or separate? Sublet or shared?

What computer hardware, software, fax, copier, accessories?

One, two, or three phone lines?

Desk, bookcases, chairs, other furniture?

Stationery, business cards, other supplies?

continued

Legal Structure

Proprietorship, partnership, S corporation, C corporation?

Support Services

Who will do bookkeeping, accounting, auditing?

Who will do typing and perform secretarial services?

Will legal services be required? If so, who will perform them?

Will other consulting staff assistance be needed?

If so, will it be provided by subcontractors or by employees?

Long-Term Goals

The outline above poses questions that pertain primarily to the first year of operation, as does the financial projection form that follows. However, after plans for the first year are complete, it's a good idea to do some long-term planning by asking how the answers to these questions will vary during years two through five of operation. These changes can then be used to form educated guesses about those succeeding years, and to develop the five-year financial projection discussed next. There may well be new services and products, new clients, expansion to other geographical areas, greater revenues, and possibly added staff during those succeeding years.

Financial Projection

This financial projection form is a simplified structure which might well suffice for most individuals starting out. It is a cash forecast only, accounting for income and expenses and cash balance. This projection does assume that there is a separate business account and that you pay yourself a salary out of that account, slowly at first.

First-Year Cash Projection

	End of First Quarter	End of Second Quarter	End of Third Quarter	End of Fourth Quarter
Cash - Beginning	30,000	20,400	20,100	20,900
Income:				
Billings		5,000	11,000	14,000
Seminars				1,000
Other				
TOTAL INCOME		5,000	11,000	15,000
Outgo:				
Own salary	5,000	5,000	10,000	15,000
Supplies	500	100	100	100
Travel	100	200	100	200
Other (computer)	4,000			
TOTAL OUTGO	9,600	5,300	10,200	15,300
Cash - End of Qtr.	20,400	20,100	20,900	20,600

Exercise: First-Year Cash Projection

If you want to analyze expected first-year financial results, forecast what seems most likely to you, then project the best results you could expect, and also the worst. You should use a format like the one above, though you may wish to make it more detailed, and develop different categories for Income and Outgo. Developing cash projections can help you think through not only whether to proceed with the new career option but also when to proceed.

Incidentally, if you have a computer spreadsheet program, it can be quite easy to prepare alternative projections by entering different amounts while the program computes the new totals automatically. All three projections—best, worst, and expected—might well be made a part of your written business plan, kept for review later as the future realities unfold.

Exercise: Five-Year Projection

Your business plan should include a five-year forecast of the financial results of your business. You can modify the format for the one-year projection extending the columns out for five years. This five-year estimate can also be made on the basis of the best, worst, and most likely expectations. Creating your five-year projection will raise a lot of "what if" questions in your mind, and reviewing these questions can be a healthy way of making sure your plans are deliberately thought through before you move ahead.

Setting up the Office

Setting up the office involves, first, deciding where to locate, and then equipping the office.

Deciding Where to Locate

More and more consultants, as well as other individual entrepreneurs, are finding that working out of their homes is a satisfactory arrangement. One overriding benefit of the home office is its relatively low cost. Another is the time saved by not having to commute regularly to some other location. A corollary of that benefit is that, when your day is spent in a home, blue jeans and a sweatshirt may be fine. That adds benefits of comfort, and lower wardrobe expense.

But there are many valid reasons for establishing a separate office. When the practice is one that requires frequent visits by clients, such as outplacement counseling or a financial advisor, clients may prefer to meet in an urban location. Some homes, especially apartments, may not have the space or the privacy to make an office feasible, especially if there are children in the home. Another good reason is strictly psychological; some consultants prefer to physically separate their business and home environments because they feel much more businesslike and comfortable in a traditional office environment.

Another excellent reason for having an office away from home is that there are many convenient and economical options for having an office in an urban setting without the full cost and responsibility of running the place. Many consultants share offices with other individual proprietors, such as lawyers or real estate professionals, some on a coequal basis, some on a sublet basis. Many of these arrangements can involve the common use of secretarial services, phones, copiers, and even computers. Similar to this, there are many offices available that are set up for the sole purpose of being shared, where the prime renter often arranges for the phones, secretarial services, copiers, and sometimes even conference rooms.

These arrangements can be tasteful and help foster a businesslike and professional image.

For a consultant about to venture out on his or her own, a prime consideration is cost, as it is important to keep expenditures limited until the momentum of billing and income reduces the difficulty of staying afloat. So it is usually best to start working from home unless there are overriding reasons for doing otherwise. A further reason the home office can be effective is the increasing efficiency of communications systems; with fax machines, voice mail, e-mail, mobile phones, and beepers, consultants can stay in touch with others even when away from the office for significant periods of time.

The January 1996 issue of *Mobile Office* contains an article describing how many consultants, as well as other businesspeople, are using hotel lobbies regularly as their offices. Some of these people are in town for a few days, and others just live nearby and find the hotel lobbies suitable for meeting others as well as for operating their laptop computers and mobile phones. Many hotels tolerate and even encourage this practice because it increases hotel business. Although the mobile office is not a practical arrangement for most consultants, it does indicate the increasing ease with which consultants can do business outside a traditional office.

As an aid to thinking through the pros and cons of a home office, it may be helpful to answer the questions in the following exercise.

Exercise: Home Office or Not?

Question	Yes	No	Comment
Do your clients have to visit your office frequently? Ever?			
Is your home situated for convenient visits by your clients?			
Is there space in your home suitable for an office?			
Are there distractions at home that would impair work concentration?			
Have you explored offices available on a shared basis?			

Equipping the Office

The equipment needs of independent consultants vary with the individual and any special circumstances. But most have pretty common requirements for basic furniture, phones, computer, fax, and copiers. Some may have secretarial assistance, but most beginners try to do the phone answering, typing, and computer operation themselves. That can be a great savings, which is key for most who are starting out. Further, by doing these chores yourself, you can often save time and get the work done faster. The disadvantage, of course, is that time spent in office administration lessens the time available for billable work.

Phones. Two lines are probably minimum, one for voice and one for fax. A third line may be justified if the volume of your business warrants it. Call waiting is a good idea if there is only one voice line. However, there are phone technologies that provide ways to both save money and give a professional image. By adding phone numbers, not lines, you can have distinctive rings for business calls, personal calls, and fax messages. The ring pattern can help you decide how best to handle the call, such as choosing whether or not to interrupt a business call for a personal call.

Furniture. The basics are a desk, comfortable chair, file cabinets, and bookcases. Lateral files use space the most economically. Make room for file expansion, as files tend to get filled up rapidly. To minimize file space, files should be purged periodically. One individual proprietor uses a computer imaging system to copy his paper files onto disks, then destroys the paper, which he says saves much space and makes his documents easier to find and refer to.

Computer. A computer will likely be a major part of your office equipment expense, if you do not already have one. To start, it may cost $2,000 to $3,000 for the basic hardware and software. The rapid changes in hardware and software make it hard to decide what to buy at any time. It is probably best to stay familiar with the most recent features of hardware and software available because some of these features can prove valuable to your business. Unfortunately, keeping up-to-date in computer developments takes time away from other needs of your business.

If you are not familiar or comfortable with computer operation, you may find it beneficial to attend some training sessions to get familiar with word processing and spreadsheets, and maybe later desktop publishing if you are interested in newsletter publishing.

Picking a Name   Selecting a name for the consulting organization is not the most important thing in getting a business underway, but it does influence how others will perceive your business. So it is desirable to give it some thought. Simpler names are usually best and can be the easiest to decide on.

There are five alternative approaches to naming your business, each has its advantages and disadvantages. You may choose a descriptive name, an abstract name, or your own name, perhaps with "Associates" or "Group," "Co.," "Inc.," or "Consulting" added. There are some variations for each of these categories.

Descriptive Name   Examples (hypothetical) of descriptive names are:

New York Information Systems Associates

Marketing Consultants, Inc.

Ajax Strategic Planners

Jones Outplacement Service Co.

Descriptive names have one advantage: they convey the firm's function and imply expertise in the area indicated. So, someone seeking a planner might well call up a firm with the word "planner" in its name as a first step in investigating that type of service.

One disadvantage is that descriptive names hinder flexibility. If after a time the planning firm develops a marketing consulting service, the firm's name no longer covers the full scope of its operation. There is also a more likely possibility of a conflict with some other organization's name. To some, a descriptive name seems more commercial and less professional than names which emphasize the names of the firm's principals.

Abstract Name   Hypothetical examples of abstract names are these:

The Red and Blue Service Organization

ABC Institute

The disadvantage of abstract names is that they don't immediately indicate the nature of your business, which may cause you to lose prospective clients who are unaware of, or confused about, what you do.

There seems to be no benefit to such a type of name

except that it does identify your business and set it apart from other organizations. These names also are not impaired if and when the function or scope of a firm is broadened or altered.

Person's Name Plus "Associates" or "Group"

Examples of this category of names are the following:

The Jones Consulting Group, Inc.

William W. Williams Associates

Arthur A. Abraham and Associates, Inc.

Shirley S. Shermon Group

The term "associates" and "group" are intended to indicate that the firm is more than a solo practitioner. Many consultants who have one or a few employees or regular subcontractors use these terms to describe their organizations.

But a large number of individual consultants who practice primarily alone also use terms like these. Most of these individuals do, with some frequency, secure engagements which require more than one person, sometimes because of the specialty needed and sometimes because of the work volume and schedule. These individuals typically have a network of peers who assist them on projects. The terms "associates" and "group" give recognition to that ability to expand forces when the need arises.

Person's Name Plus "Co.," "Inc.," or "Consulting"

Adding "Co.," "Inc.," or "Consulting" creates names like the following:

McKinsey & Co., Inc.

Booz, Allen & Hamilton, Inc.

Abramson Consulting

Jones, Jacobs, & Jeremy Co., Inc.

These names are certainly easy to decide on, and they have a professional tone. The first two are large, well-respected consulting companies and were established at a time when this style was preferred by consultants. They seem professional, as do the names of many legal and auditing firms.

The disadvantage of these names is that they are a bit dull, unimaginative, and old fashioned. They do set a conservative tone, which may or may not be the firm's desired image.

Person's Name Only

A few consultants use no firm name and operate under their own names only. The absence of a firm name indicates that the person is, indeed, acting as a solo consultant, and prefers not to infer that the business includes a staff of assistants.

Frequency of Different Name Styles

A review of the firm names in the member directory of the Institute of Management Consultants showed that the proportions of names in each style are as follows:

23%	Descriptive Name
16%	Abstract Name
20%	Person's Name Plus "Associates" or "Group"
31%	Person's Name Plus "Co.," "Inc.," or "Consulting"
10%	Person's Name Only
100%	

Legal Clearance for Name

Whatever name you select for your business, you need to get it approved and registered by the county or state office concerned. That is unless you do business under your own unadulterated name. Even if you only add "Co." after your name, banks will not set up an account in that name without proper governmental approval.

Structure: Proprietorship, Partnership, Corporation

There are three basic business structures in the United States: proprietorship, partnership, and corporation. Each is regulated by the states as far as the rules of operation, but each also has different tax consequences, both federal and state. The features of each category are explained next, along with the pros and cons, and certain variations of the partnership and corporation options.

Proprietorship

Proprietorship is the simplest of the three. You and your business are one and the same for legal and tax purposes. Your business assets are your assets, and your business liabilities are your liabilities. The business income and expenses are explained on IRS Schedule C of Form 1040 as part of your personal tax return. If you operate under your name, there is no need to get clearance or to register your name.

The advantages are that there are no papers or clearances needed to get started and no periodic reports to anyone other than the tax authorities. You alone run the business and need not share decisions or information with anyone. Also, business losses can sometimes offset personal income tax expenses.

There are two disadvantages to proprietorship: (1) any business liabilities are your personal liabilities—there is no liability protection as with a corporation; and (2) you are required to pay the equivalent of the employer's and employee's shares of Social Security as a self-employment tax.

Partnership

When two or more individuals make an agreement to do business together without incorporating, it is a partnership. The agreement should specify how the profits and losses will be shared and how much each partner will invest in the business. The partnership business is not taxed as such; business income is reported on a Schedule K-1 of Form 1065, a copy of which is then filed with each partner's personal return, on Schedule E of Form 1040.

The partners control the business, which is a private matter between them. No special reports are required, so it's easier to form than a corporation. Financing is easier to arrange than with a proprietorship. And partnership losses can offset personal income taxes.

But the main disadvantage is that liabilities of the business can become the responsibility of the individual partners; there is no liability protection as with a corporation.

However, there are limited partnerships in which the limited partners are shielded from liability, though they have no control over the business affairs. But the general partners have no liability protection in a limited partnership.

Corporations

There are a few variations of the corporate structure. A "C corporation," named after the Internal Revenue Service's Subchapter C, is a normal, for-profit incorporated organization. An S corporation, reviewed in the next section, has several benefits and limitations often suitable to smaller and newer organizations.

Corporations are legal entities owned by stockholders, whose ownership is represented by shares of stock in the corporation. A corporation is guided by bylaws and run by officers who report to the board of directors. A corporation is established by filing of articles of incorporation with the secretary of state where the corporation is formed. C corporations' earnings are taxed twice; first the corporation as such pays taxes on profits earned in the year, then stockholders pay taxes on the dividends they earned.

A main benefit of the corporate structure is that the stockholders are not liable for the obligations or actions of the corporate entity. Corporations can secure additional funds by issuing more stock, as well as via loans. A corporation can endure indefinitely, while partnerships and proprietorships cannot outlast their principals. And corporations, as separate entities, can be sold. Finally, being a corporation may strengthen the public's perception of a consultant as an established business.

There are several disadvantages to the corporate form. It takes time, effort, and expense to establish a corporation, and privacy is impaired because the filing documents are public. Control is diverse, shared by all stockholders, and the stockholders may not offset corporate losses against the personal taxes they owe. And, for C corporations, the double taxation feature can be a significant disadvantage.

S Corporations

S corporations have one main advantage over C corporations: there is no double taxation. As with partnerships, the corporation itself does not pay a tax; income is passed through to the owners who pay tax on their personal income tax forms. And the S corporation provides an important advantage over the partnership: the shareholders are protected against the corporation's liabilities.

Checklist

The following checklist is to help you review the issues discussed in this chapter as they relate to your consulting plans or practice.

	Yes	No
Do you have a strong desire to be an independent consultant?		
Can you arrange for consulting work on a part-time basis?		
Do you have experience as a consulting firm member?		
Is it feasible to secure consulting from your former employer?		
Can you secure consulting work from a recently downsized company?		
Have you prepared a written business plan?		
Does the plan cover points mentioned in the outline?		
Does your cash projection indicate sufficient beginning cash?		
Does your firm name project the image you want?		
If you select a structure other than proprietorship, are there good reasons for the extra cost and inconvenience?		

How to Perform Problem-Solving and Advisory Services

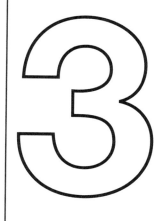

A large part of what most consultants do consists of helping to resolve problems of one sort or another for organizations or individuals. Consultants may also counsel clients on how to manage their organizations and advise groups on how to improve their performance. Typical consulting services would be designing a parts warehouse, developing a plan to merchandise a new product, providing career advice to executives, training a new sales staff, or constructing a computerized materials control system.

All of these activities are things that might be done by an employee. But a consultant may be preferable when the need is temporary or the employee staff does not have the required time or skills. So a consultant is retained to do the work on a contract basis.

What makes you a consultant is your relation to the person or organization that pays you, not the type of work that you do. This book does not explain how to do the job that is your speciality, be it engineering, human resources, or whatever. It does cover matters relating to your relationship with the clients who retain and pay you.

Therefore, this chapter will review how to make proposals, how to negotiate consulting contracts, how to set fees, how to analyze clients' problems, how to work with the client's personnel, and how to make reports and presentations. Those are the sorts of things all consultants do, regardless of their specialty.

A large proportion of consultants, in addition to performing problem solving and advisory services for clients, conduct seminars, make speeches, and write newsletters, articles, and books. These functions fit well with the problem-solving and advisory role for three reasons: (1) they help consultants maintain an image of expertness in their field, (2) they generate contacts which can lead to referrals and more business, (3) they produce revenue. These writing and speaking services are discussed further in Chapter 4.

How to Make Proposals

Proposals can be made at several levels of formality: (1) to confirm understandings about a project based on informal discussions about what the client wants and how the consultant would do it, (2) in response to a Request for Proposal from a government agency, (3) in response to a Request for Proposal from a business or other nongovernmental organization, and (4) to acquire legal advice and wording because of some special requirements of the proposal or contract.

Proposals Based on Informal Discussions

Some of the better consulting engagements develop when a relationship of some respect is established between a potential client and the consultant. Perhaps you have just finished a project, and your client is exploring another piece of work you may do. Or the discussion may develop from a mutual acquaintance who knew of the client's problem and suggested that you might be a person to solve it.

When a discussion about a potential engagement begins with mutual interest and trust, the potential client generally reviews the problem, how it came about, what should be done about it, and when. Then the consultant usually discusses possible approaches, similar past experiences, and the suggested solution. The consultant might talk about data the client's people would have to furnish, client staff to be consulted, and similar issues.

Then, when there seems to be a general agreement on whether and how to approach the issue, the consultant might well say, "Why don't I give you a proposal on this to help you think about it and decide." This proposal would be written for that stated reason, and also because, with sizable jobs, the consultant knows that the client may have to secure the approval of a superior or possibly of a committee. If a client verbally accepts your plan, fine, but it is still a good idea to confirm the details in writing so as to avoid any subsequent misunderstanding about the agreement.

A proposal of this type should be short, one page or two at the most, though there may be attachments. It should cover all of the important points, especially those that might cause any misunderstanding, such as deadlines, cost, and client's responsibilities. Here is an outline of the features of such a proposal:

Heading. Normal business letterhead, with addressee and a descriptive subject.

Opening. The first paragraph would say something like "This will confirm our discussions of (date)" and then give a one or two sentence summary.

Objective. A brief statement in general terms of what the client wants.

Action Steps. A list, maybe in bullet fashion, of the sequential actions you plan to take. This should also include a statement of when you will submit periodic progress reports.

Beneficial Results. This can be part of the selling function. A brief statement of the worthwhile results the client wants, as well of any additional by-product benefits you anticipate you will accomplish.

Client's Responsibilities. These can be the time specified interviewees are expected to spend, documents to be made available, maybe office facilities, and sometimes even secretarial services.

Time and Costs. This should be a short statement of your rate per day, the number of expected days, and the total bill. It should also include the billing cycle; is it biweekly or monthly? Payment deadlines can be explained here or under Client Responsibilities. You can include a maximum number of days if the scope and terms of the agreement are not changed.

Conclusion. This can be a brief general statement of the value the client may expect to receive from the engagement, and the fact that you are looking forward to working on it. And it should include something specific like "Please let me know when you would like to start this project," to get a response and, hopefully, an oral acceptance of the agreement.

Your Qualifications and Credentials. This is not necessary if the client has verbally accepted your offer, which the letter is confirming. But if the client you have been negotiating with has to get someone else's approval, this feature would be in order. It can usually be done as an attachment to the letter, through copies of a brochure about your firm or a curriculum vitae or resume of each individual who will work on the job.

Some may wish to add a place for the client to sign to confirm acceptance of the proposal. This is fine, but it does make your proposal look more like a formal contract than a friendly agreement.

Exercise: Proposal Preparation

Prepare a proposal for an actual or hypothetical engagement using the outline just presented.

Response to a Government Request for Proposal (RFP)

RFPs from federal, state, or local government agencies are issued to get competitive bids on projects the agencies need undertaken. This means that if you are responding to an RFP, you must feel confident that you have a good chance of being accepted as the best of the group of competitors who submit bids. Your proposal must be a marketing document that convinces the agency you are more worthy of the job than your competitors.

It takes quite a bit of time to prepare government proposals, especially because they must be top notch to have a reasonable chance for success. So it is not cost effective to develop RFPs unless there seems to be a likelihood of winning.

The ways for positioning yourself to receive RFPs are covered in Chapter 5.

The federal and other governments have established regulations to fairly and honestly select vendors, and to avoid temptations in bureaucracies to play favorites or accept favors. These rules generally work quite well in fostering genuine competition, but they have the drawback of requiring considerable paperwork and time to process the documents.

The two things necessary for success with government RFPs are (1) give them exactly what they ask for, and (2) use every opportunity to mention reasons for accepting you and your firm over your competitors. RFPs usually ask for a lot of information, including your costs (which make many avoid responding altogether), and a clear, complete explanation of your proposed approach. The RFP will contain a submission date, and if the proposal is not received on time it will be thrown out unless, for some reason, you have been able to receive a time extension.

To use the proposal as a marketing document, include all pertinent data about your accomplishments, and those of your staff, on matters akin to the RFP project purpose. Describe these accomplishments and their beneficial results, preferably numerically measurable results. Be specific, brief, and concrete, avoiding adjectives and adverbs. Those accomplishments show better than any other way your ability to fulfill the agency's project objective, whatever that may be. If the project involves research into a technical specialty and you have relevant credentials—advanced degrees, teaching experience, publications, or awards in the subject area—emphasize that information.

Competitive bidding does not mean necessarily that the award will always go to the lowest bidder. Most government organizations' rules provide that proposals be evaluated on some weighted subjective scale. The criteria may be such things as qualifications of consultants, creativity of the approach, time needed to complete the job, clarity and completeness of proposal, and other factors that may be evaluated by a committee or team. Rules might specify that the award goes to the lowest bid of the top three as rated on the subjective analysis, or some such process.

RFPs from business entities have a few elements in common with government RFPs, but generally are less rigid.

Response to a Business Request for Proposal

RFPs are issued by business organizations, not because they have to conform to some regulation (unless the job is a subcontract of a government project), but because they genuinely want to find who best can fulfill their needs. They want to know which consultants might help them solve their problems, what approaches those consultants would suggest, and what cost and time would be required for each one. They also want to know which consultants appear best qualified by education, training, and experience.

In making their award decisions, businesses usually do not have the elaborate evaluation schemes that government agencies do. More likely, the decision maker has one or two subordinates review the proposals, maybe talk with leading contenders, and then present recommendations to the decision maker for approval.

As with government RFPs, it is important to give the data the requestor asked for in a clear and convincing way. A proposal is a sales document, so it should be written in a way that makes recipients view you favorably. That means showing in the best light the pertinent accomplishments of the people who would do the work, dramatizing the beneficial and measurable results achieved for others in matters similar to the project at hand.

Government agencies issuing RFPs occasionally interview leading contenders before making their decisions. Discussions are more likely with business RFPs than with government RFPs. It is often possible and desirable to ask for a meeting before preparing the proposal, saying that you want to make sure you understand their requirements and expectations. Such meetings can give you an opportunity to become aware of some client needs or desires that are not fully covered in the RFP, giving you the advantage of preparing a proposal with values not considered by competitors who have not met with the client. And it also gives you an opportunity to give the client a feeling of your own competence and confidence, and—very important—a sense that you would be the type of person they would feel comfortable dealing with. That personal chemistry is something that cannot be conveyed on paper very well, yet it may be one of the most influential deciding factors.

Lawyer-Assisted Contracts

There are many situations where it is necessary or desirable to get attorneys involved. These include consulting projects of long duration and those that involve sale and use of equipment, implementation and continuing support, development of computer programs that raise issues of copyright and perpetual availability, or other projects in which a client's attorney will be involved.

Such situations involve complex obligations and rights of both parties, and it is important that all concerned clearly understand the agreement terms. That is where lawyers can provide a useful service by being catalysts to make sure the issues and implications are fully thought out; the writing down and several reviews of the proposed terms can help accomplish that goal.

Usually such situations start with a general agreement between client and consultant about what will be done. Then one of the attorneys will put the terms in legal format, and the draft will be reviewed and amended several times by the consultant and client and their attorneys. This is all part of the constructive "thinking through" process. That process often raises points of disagreement. The attorneys can sometimes help mediate and resolve these conflicts.

How to Negotiate Contracts

The object of all negotiations is to make an arrangement which benefits both parties, in this case client and consultant—so-called "win-win" situations. Anything less than mutual benefit is unsatisfactory professionally and unpleasant personally.

The best way to negotiate a contract is through informal discussion, described earlier. When potential clients have a problem or project, they meet with you because they know you have the skills to resolve such matters. Then in your meeting, the client explains the problem and you both discuss ways you could resolve the matter. You ask questions, the client explains further, and eventually a proposed solution emerges.

That discussion then, if all goes well, becomes a friendly understanding of what the problem is and how you can resolve it, followed by an offer on your part to put it all in writing as the next step in getting moving on the project. Putting the proposal in writing helps to ensure that clients get what they want, you get what you want, and everyone is happy with the result.

In situations where you meet with the potential client as a result of a business RFP, you usually do not have the benefit of an established, friendly relationship going for you. The client may have received appealing proposals from some of your competitors. The client may like your proposal but think it could be done at a lower cost, faster, or with some other approach. You may then offer to amend your proposal by leaving out some of the less important steps, or speed it up, or modify the proposed method to one more acceptable to the client.

These negotiations still remain ostensibly friendly, but each party is evaluating the other and guessing what may be acceptable to the other or how much the other may yield on a particular issue. With some give and take, an oral agreement usually can be reached in these discussions, with you offering to submit a written revision of your proposal reflecting the changes you have mutually agreed to.

As in other interpersonal relationships discussed in this book, being able to listen carefully is important in negotiations. Asking questions about why clients feel as they do, and trying to listen carefully to figure out what may really be in the back of their minds, is helpful. Asking questions properly gives the other person the feeling that you are interested. And the answers may enlighten you as to what is possible and give you clues as to how to achieve it.

How to Set Fees

You should set fees at a level you can reasonably get for the services you offer. That fee must take into account competitive rates and what you need to cover your costs.

In starting a consulting business, it is natural and reasonable to charge a bit less than what you know or believe your competitors' rates to be. That is fine up to a point, but remember that clients regard your pricing as a measure of your own assessment of the value of your services. It is said that "if the price is cheap, it can't be any good."

Actually, however, the ultimate low pricing strategy worked for one consultant getting started, but in an unusual way. With no success in securing clients initially, the consultant, trying to establish his business, offered to do a job free for a client providing that the client would give him a good recommendation if the client was pleased with the result. This arrangement did prove helpful in getting the consultant underway in his new career as it broke that barrier of prospective clients asking, "Whom have you done consulting work for before?"

Competitive Factors

Competitive forces will probably be the primary determinant of your fee structure. It may be difficult to find out what others in your community are charging for the type of service you offer. Asking your competitors is generally not feasible. If you happen to know one or two of your competitors' clients personally, you may sometimes be able to get an idea of their billing rates through them.

The exhibit on billing rates shown next lists what the Association of Management Consulting Firms determined to be average fees for their members. Those firms tend to be larger, well known and well regarded, with reputations that enable them to command generous rates. But it does show what some firms charge for typical management consulting specialties. You will note that the ratio of billing rates to base salaries ranges from about 3.3 to 1 to 7.4 to 1, compared to the 2 to 1 suggested as minimum for a beginning independent consultant.

Billing Rates—ACME Survey

Hourly Billing Rates for Employees Earning the Following Base Salaries	Strategic Planning	Production Management	Human Resources	Health Care Consulting	Multiple Consulting Specialties	Other Types of Consulting
$35,000	$83	$125	$72	$78	$80	$98
$60,000	$138	$150	$119	$118	$138	$170
$75,000	$170	$160	$150	$150	$170	$198
$125,000	$250	$200	$225	$225	$235	$285
Standard Hourly Billing Rates for:						
Senior Partners or Equivalent	$200	$193	$225	$263	$234	$275
Junior Partners or Equivalent	$270	$175	$168	$180	$200	$245
Senior Management Consultants	$200	$150	$125	$150	$173	$190
Management Consultants	$145	$125	$100	$105	$137	$150
Entry-Level Consultants	$110	N/A	$85	$93	$105	$100
Research Associates	$78	N/A	$60	$50	$65	$53

Source: *1995 ACME Survey of U.S. Key Management Information*, Association of Management Consulting Firms (ACME), New York.

Cost and Overhead

One rule of thumb might be to take what you could expect as a salary and at least double it. It shows that a salary rate of $1,500 a week, or $300 a day, would be the basis for a $600 per diem billing rate at the minimum. These are the computations:

$1500 a week, or $78,000 a year

= $300 a day

+ 40% fringe benefits such as for medical, vacations, holidays, pension

= $420 a day

+ 25% to allow for 1 day a week marketing and administration, assuming 4 days a week are billed

= $525 a day

+ $75 a day or $15,000 per year for office and over-head expenses and profits

= $600 per diem billing rate

÷ 8 hour day

= $75 per hour billing rate

The Cost and Overhead rate calculation of $75 per hour is far below the range of from $150 to $198 per hour in the ACME survey for employees earning the same annual base salary of $75,000. This wide difference indicates the opportunity for independent consultants to grow in reputation, increase their income and still be competitive with the larger, older, more prestigious firms. That ACME report listed 45 member firms which included such well-known organizations as:

Coopers & Lybrand Consultants

Deloitte & Touche

EDS Management Consulting Services

IBM Consulting Group

Towers Perrin

How Flexible to Be

There are often questions of whether to adjust rates for big jobs, slow periods, or under pressure from a prospective client.

Some consultants, once they establish a daily or hourly rate, set that fixed rate for every job, no matter what the circumstances. That policy has the advantage of being consistent and evenhanded. It also indicates that you are confident about your fee and are going to stick with it.

But that rigid rule is contrary to the idea that rates are competitive and, therefore, may vary from time to time and client to client. A moderate approach is to be generally firm but occasionally flexible and willing to make adjustments when unusual or important circumstances warrant, such as taking on a relatively long-term assignment at a modestly lower than usual rate.

Many consultants have reported that as their businesses gained momentum, and their popularity grew, they gradually increased their billing rates. This is a reasonable way of adjusting to a more favorable competitive position, and of being rewarded for performing effective consulting work. As your reputation grows, so will your fees.

The next two exercises will help you estimate the billing rates of your leading competitors, and the minimum rate you need to meet your expected salary, based on the analyses above.

Exercise: Estimating Competitive Billing Rates

Circle the Base Salary (per "Billing Rates—ACME Survey," page 47) which is closest to the rate you expect to achieve:	Base Salary $35,000 $60,000 $75,000 $125,000
Enter the hourly billing rate for your field based on the ACME survey:	Hourly Billing Rate:
Strategic Planning	$
Production Management	$
Human Resources	$
Health Care Consulting	$
Multiple Consulting Specialties	$
Other Types of Consulting	$

This exercise may help you visualize what leading consultants in your specialy command for fees, as well as the types of billing rates that might be the highest attainable for you in the long run.

Exercise: Estimating Minimum Feasible Billing Rates

$ _____ a week, or $ _____ a year (expected base salary)

= $ _____ a day

+ _____ % fringe benefits such as for medical, vacations, holidays, pension

= $ _____ a day

+ _____ % to allow for _____ day(s) a week marketing and administration,

assuming _____ days a week are billed

= $ _____ a day

+ $ _____ a day or $ _____ per year for office and overhead expenses and

profit

= $ _____ per diem billing rate

÷ 8 hour day

= $ _____ per hour billing rate

This computation of estimates should give you a reasoned minimum billing rate to cover your expected salary or take-home pay, fringe benefits, office and other overhead expenses, and an allowance for the time needed for marketing activities.

How to Solve Problems

Typical consulting engagements involve resolving some problem. Although your exact approach will depend upon your profession, certain concepts are helpful to all consultants in carrying out their engagements. These concepts are reviewed next and then illustrated through hypothetical example.

The broad steps are to gather the pertinent facts, analyze those findings to determine the real problem and its causes, then apply creative thinking to come up with a practical solution.

Gathering the facts usually involves reviewing records and interviewing people responsible for the related activities. The interviews should uncover relevant facts, as well as the views of the people concerned regarding the causes and possible solutions. Asking the right questions, listening carefully, and showing an interest in the people you interview are essential. From that fact gathering, it may be clear that there is only one reasonable solution. There may seem to be several possible solutions, with a variety of pros and cons to consider. If no solution is readily apparent, you can step aside and use your imagination to try to devise some solution entirely unthought of previously. In this creative process, brainstorming with one or more of your associates can sometimes help. Then, after you have weighed the possible solutions and determined which ones best fit the client's need, the final step is to put your reasoned judgment in a report, clearly explaining the logic behind your recommendations.

Suppose you have been hired to determine the causes and recommended solutions for an inordinately high number of consumer complaints for a product. You would need to gather records of the numbers and types of complaints, and interview people responsible for factors affecting product quality—such as purchasing, production, and quality control. A few of these people might be defensive, fearing that you may uncover and report deficiencies in their performance. You must therefore evaluate their responses in the light of their biases and worries. In this case, you will probably recommend multiple causes and multiple solutions. Common sense might determine the recommendations you make. Your independent judgment and solutions supported by documented facts would be the values you would bring to this client.

How to Work with the Client's Personnel

Three key things are important to remember in dealing with client personnel. First, your success depends on their cooperation and help. Second, they report to their superiors, not to you. Third, they may be hesitant and defensive if they think your comments about them, maybe unfavorable ones, will be passed along to the individuals who have engaged you.

To gain their respect it is helpful to be courteous, considerate, sincerely interested in them and their ideas, and willing to listen. These attitudes will do a great deal to overcome what is often a cautious or reluctant stance on their part. If you do encounter hesitation, it can help to lead the discussion into areas in which personnel can speak positively about their job and performance.

Keep your ears open for ideas clients' personnel may have. Many interviewees are delighted to have someone who is willing to listen to their point of view. They may have proposed some of these ideas before and had them rejected. Other ideas they may have kept to themselves because they thought their superiors would not be willing to consider them. In either case, any constructive ideas are worth considering. They may be suitable to build into your consulting recommendations, often because you may see ways around what were previously judged to be obstacles. Always give full credit to anyone who suggests an idea you use or report as worth considering. A maxim to remember is "It's amazing what you can get done if you don't care who gets the credit." Besides, treating client personnel fairly may help you in subsequent dealings with them.

One pitfall to avoid, which frequently happens when a consultant talks to an interviewee, is a statement beginning with "Between you and me," "Confidentially," or "Off the record." Encouraging such relationships conflicts with the primary loyalty due to the persons who have retained you. Should you receive a worthy idea this way, encourage the interviewee to let you regard it as on the record.

How to Make Reports and Presentations

The usual types of written reports consultants produce are progress reports during the engagement, and final reports of the study conclusions and recommendations. Final written reports are sometimes supplemented by oral presentations to those concerned. Oral progress reports are usually made informally on projects of any significant duration. Presentations may be called for when you submit a proposal, to explain to and discuss with interested client personnel the issues and consulting plan for the project.

Periodic Progress Reports

With engagements of a month or more, it is a good idea to submit written reports periodically to the client, whether they are asked for or not. Providing such reports makes you appear professional and open and above board, and it helps prevent possible subsequent misunderstandings.

Usually, of course, there are frequent or daily discussions with clients which keep them informed of your progress. But even so, weekly, semimonthly, or monthly written progress reports have several values. They confirm to the client that appropriate progress is being made, and they help justify the bills which you may be issuing with similar frequency. And they give you an opportunity to explain any significant problems or unexpected developments you encounter, so the client is made aware of matters that may alter the course of action originally set.

One progress format that is popular with clients is to cover these headings: *Actions During the Period, Findings and Observations, Problems Encountered* if any, and *Next Steps.* The *Actions During the Period* section should normally be closely related to the planned steps outlined in your proposal. *Findings and Observations* includes any facts you discovered that may interest the client or that support your recommendations. The *Problems Encountered* section includes such matters as an interviewee's absence due to illness, needed records that are missing, or some condition that is contrary to the assumptions made when the proposal was prepared. *Next Steps* merely outlines your planned actions during the next period, or other steps to be taken because of problems you encountered.

Progress reports should be brief, normally less than one page. They need not go into much detail. If frequent or daily discussions occur with clients, they already understand the points in the report, which is desirable. Progress reports should offer written confirmation of what the client already knows.

Final Project Reports

Clients usually expect written reports at the completion of problem-solving and similar types of consulting projects. These reports can follow an outline similar to the proposal outline, and they must be related to the proposal substantively. The proposal said what you were going to do and the benefits expected; now the final report states what you actually did, and the beneficial results that actually were, or will be, accomplished.

An outline of a final report for a typical consulting project is as follows:

Introductory Paragraph

Objectives. A restatement of the objectives as presented in your proposal, or as subsequently amended in oral or written agreements.

Steps Taken. A list of the steps actually taken, with an explanation of any deviations from the proposal steps.

Findings and Observations. A summary of the facts and conditions uncovered of significance to the client, especially those that support your recommendations.

Recommendations. Statements of the new policies, procedures, and actions proposed to remedy the problems stated in the objectives, along with explanations of the reasoning behind each recommendation.

Beneficial Results. Ideally these are the results the proposal said would be achieved. Often there are benefits from the study which were not foreseen in the proposal, and these should be included too. If any results anticipated in the proposal are not included, the reasons why should be stated here.

Attachments. Often it is useful to attach data, such as schedules of facts gathered or analyses, which will support the report's conclusions.

Enclosing your reports in report covers helps foster a professional appearance. These folders may have your name, or the firm's name, logo, and address printed thereon. An appropriate cover letter should accompany the report, either inside or outside the folder. If the engagement has uncovered other areas where your services might be beneficial, or where you might give further assistance in implementing your recommendations, the cover letter is a good place to suggest to the client that you are willing to assist in these additional ways.

Presentations

Oral presentations are quite regularly made at the end of important problem solving or analysis engagements, and they are made often as part of proposal submissions and as interim progress reports. The effectiveness of your oral presentations can significantly influence your success in gaining acceptance for proposals and report recommendations. The next chapter discusses ways to be effective as a speaker because many consultants use public speaking to supplement their major consulting efforts and as part of their marketing programs.

In this chapter, the "how to" speaking suggestions are limited to presentations, progress reports, and proposals. The main points to remember are that

- oral presentations should tie in closely with the written reports on the same matters,

- carefully prepared visual aids can help ensure that the audience clearly understands your points, and

- preparation and possibly even rehearsing may help assure the issues are well planned and thought through before you make a presentation.

It is also best to try to arrange for the client's decision maker and other interested high-level personnel to attend so that your words are heard directly by those who influence the client's decisions. As part of the networking process, these people are key for providing referrals and steering business your way.

Checklist The following checklist will help you review the issues in this chapter as they apply to your consulting practice or plans.

	Yes	No
Are informal proposals kept short?		
Do informal proposals cover the objective, action steps, results, time and costs, and client's responsibilities?		
Do government proposals cover all of each RFP's requirements?		
Do proposals from RFPs use every opportunity to make sales points?		
Do proposals from RFPs contain pertinent measurable accomplishments?		
Have efforts been made to meet with originators of business RFPs?		
Do computer client agreements contain proper legal protection for both parties?		
Is "listening carefully" incorporated in all meetings with client personnel and with potential clients?		
Are billing rates set adequately to cover overhead, benefits, and marketing time?		
Do interviews with client personnel consider their loyalties, fears, and other feelings?		
Is credit always given to those who suggest worthy ideas?		
Are interviewees requests for confidentiality diplomatically avoided?		
Are regular written progress reports submitted to clients who do not ask for them?		
Are written progress reports brief and to the point?		
Do final reports cover adequately the points in the proposal?		
Do final reports suggest further follow-up work?		
Are efforts made to have decision makers and other important client personnel present at final report meetings?		

Writing, Speaking, and Other Services and Products

Writing and speaking are occasional or frequent parts of most independent consulting practices, for several good reasons. Writing and speaking can reinforce consultants' reputations for being leaders or authorities in their specialties. Writing and speaking activities are usually well documented and publicized and thereby broaden the awareness among potential clients of your capabilities and available services.

Thus, writing and speaking can help in the critical marketing of problem-solving and advisory services, usually the bread and butter of consulting. For some, writing and speaking are the predominant consulting activity. But their value works the other way too. Problem-solving and advisory functions give consultants hands-on experience and exposure to practical matters in their specialities. That experience, in turn, furnishes consultants with facts and ideas they may well write or speak about. For example, a consultant might write or speak about some problem he or she has resolved with special success, something that others would be interested in reading or hearing about. So the problem solving feeds and supports the writing and speaking activities, as well as vice versa.

The writing can take any of several forms. Many consultants use newsletters to help merchandise their service, and some publish newsletters for revenue. Writing can be produced in book form, articles, or advice columns in technical or business publications.

Speaking formats can be talks at professional association monthly meetings or annual conferences, before local business groups, or seminars put on by the consultant or by commercial training businesses. Several consultants have regular, continuing teaching roles at colleges and universities.

Other products and services include audio and video cassettes of speeches and presentations which are sold as a subsidiary function of the regular consulting business. One consultant who speaks often always carries a micro-cassette recorder to tape the talks, then sells copies to anyone who wants to purchase one, and sometimes gives them away as a merchandising tactic, like a free sample.

Most of the writing and speaking activities and other by-products have the benefit of producing revenue. This revenue supplements consultants' income from problem-solving and advice services, with the added value of evening out some of the financial peaks and valleys that often go with the "regular" consulting services.

All of these writing, speaking, and other product options will be discussed along with their benefits, and how to develop, prepare, and merchandise them.

Writing

There are many types of writing topics. One approach is to describe a successful new strategy or process. Another is to explain research that sheds light on issues of interest. Or you can write about things that are common knowledge but put them together, as in a textbook, with superior organization, completeness, and understanding, tailoring them to a distinctive audience, or using an easier-to-understand presentation style.

Discussed next are ways to find publishers, how to prepare your material, and newsletter issues. As with problem-solving types of consulting, getting the second writing assignment is easier than securing the first. Your reputation from a successful first writing project may prompt the publishers to request a second one, and so on. Momentum helps. Getting articles published is easier than publishing books, and newsletters are things you can publish yourself with relative ease.

Where and How to Find Publishers for Books

There are three ways to get a publisher for books: use an agent, contact editors directly, or publish it yourself. Any librarian can lead you to books listing publishers or agents and their general fields of interest. R. R. Bowker's *Literary Market Place*, "the directory of the book publishing industry," includes much information about book publishers, agents, and related data.

Before contacting agents or editors, however, it is a good idea to draft a statement of information they will need, including a summary of the subject to be covered, what is distinctive about it, what types of readers it would interest, and why. Those matters should be clear in your mind before you converse with or write to agents or publishers. It is also best to have a draft of one chapter.

With potential agents, try to phone and ask about their interest in the proposed work; then proceed from there. With publishers, it is best to prepare a one-page letter covering the points just listed. Then send the letter to ten or so of the publishers that seem most suitable. It's unlikely that you will hear from them for a while, so it is worthwhile to give each one a call and ask them if they have any questions about your proposal. You will probably be told they haven't reviewed it yet, so say that you'll give them another call at some future date.

Then keep following up until you do get a response from each publisher. If no favorable results come from those letters, you can then send out the letter to ten or more other publishers. If you have received feedback from editors, those comments may help you revise the letter or sample chapter to overcome obstacles the editor may have pointed out. Keep working at it until you make a deal.

Do-it-yourself publishing is another option that has become more practical with the word processing and desktop publishing computer programs available today. With a good desktop program and a modestly priced personal computer, it is relatively easy to produce so-called "camera ready copy," that is, copy that a printer can photograph and then print and bind to complete the book.

There are two ways of marketing books you have self-published: by doing it yourself or using a distributor. Doing your own selling involves creating a flyer and other sales material, and mailing it to lists of prospects. You can obtain a list of prospects from professional associations or create one using the yellow pages. There are also companies who can create tailor-made lists using many criteria such as industry or geographical area. Marketing on your own has the advantage of being under your direct control. But you have to bear the costs of creating lists, flyers, and mailing material, buying postage, and the expense of housing the book inventory and mailing books out. However, there is no sharing of the profit with a book distributor as with the second approach. You may be able also to sell the book directly to retailers like Barnes & Noble if the book is of interest to the general public or to well-populated groups like computer users.

The second way of marketing your book is to use a distributor who will handle the book advertising, warehousing, and shipping. Some companies specialize in selling books produced by others, and other publishing companies are sometimes willing to take on self-published books. The following list may be helpful in this regard:

Book Wholesalers and Distributors

ACP Distributors
105 Pine Road
Sewickley, PA 15143

Atlantis Distributors
1725 Carondelet
New Orleans, LA 70130

Bookslinger
2163 Ford Parkway
St. Paul, MN 55116

COSMEP/South
Box 209
Carrboro, NC 27510

New England Small Press Association
45 Hillcrest Place
Amherst, MA 01002

New York State Small Press Association
Box 1624
Radio City Station
New York, NY 10001

Plains Distribution Service
Box 3112, Room 500, Block 6
620 Main Street
Fargo, ND 58102

These are organizations that distribute others' books. Also, some established publishers occasionally distribute others' books. St. Martin's Press is one that does so, and there are others.

Source: Taken from *How to Succeed as an Independent Consultant* by Herman Holtz. © 1993. John Wiley & Sons, Inc. Reprinted by permission of John Wiley & Sons, Inc.

R.R. Bowker's *Literary Market Place*, cited earlier, also has further lists of marketers for books as well as lists of companies who can print and bind books from an author's copy.

Royalties for books published by others typically are from 10 percent to 15 percent of the publisher's net sales, maybe 10 percent to 12 percent for the first 3,000 to 5,000 copies sold, and higher percentages above that. The publisher may give the author an advance of a few thousand dollars, usually part on signing the contract and part upon acceptance of the manuscript.

If you seriously are interested in getting into book publishing, you may find it helpful to contact or join the National Writers Union. At local meetings of this group, you can meet with people who have experience in dealing with agents, publishers, author contracts, royalty fees, and related matters. They also publish newsletters and other material about contract negotiation, royalty provisions, and other topics of interest to authors. Annual dues are $75 if your annual writing income is under $5,000 and up to $170 if it is over $25,000. They can be contacted at National Writers Union, 873 Broadway, Suite 203, New York, New York 10003, (212) 254–0279.

Where and How to Find Publishers for Articles

Getting articles published is a lot easier than publishing books. Most business specialties have one or several periodicals, and the computer field has an abundance of periodical publications. Many technical fields have journals, often sponsored by related associations, which cover technical matters and new developments in their areas.

Most of these periodicals are eager to find authors who can write about a new development or a particular accomplishment in their specialties. So if you have something to say that you think would be of interest to the readers of a publication, you can contact the editor in a memo, or even by phone, to propose the article and get a reaction. A memo should cover briefly the essence of what you have to say, and why you think it would interest the magazine's readers.

Possible topics are a description of a project that achieved unusually good results, an idea opposing or clarifying a point of view, a technique that may be of value to others in the profession, or an explanation of an issue that has not been covered sufficiently well in print.

Compensation usually won't be much, but it may help compensate a bit for the time you spend. Publishers of articles know that many authors, especially consultants, are compensated primarily by the publicity and recognition they get, which helps consultants in their profession.

Many publications contain one or more regular columns, which can provide information or advice. These columns typically cover some part of the specialty of the periodical, and the writers therefore do get continuing publicity as authorities in their fields. Such authorship is not easy to find, but it can provide excellent benefits to a consultant in terms of recognition and a regular modest income supplement.

Highlights of Good Writing Techniques

A number of how-to rules and techniques can help keep your writing clear and easy to understand. These principles are summarized next.

Outline. A good first step is to make an outline. Try to think of things you plan to say, then arrange them in a logical sequence. This outline process often can be improved by drafting an outline, setting it aside for a few days, and then reviewing and revising it. This waiting and review usually brings forth more and better ideas and an improved arrangement.

Headings. Having many headings is a good idea. The outline forms a basis for the headings. The headings help readers follow your train of thought as they read the piece through. Headings are of great value to someone scanning the work to find a part of particular interest, or to get the gist of it. They also encourage the writer to put the piece together logically.

Introduction. A careful introduction that summarizes what you are going to say helps readers follow your reasoning throughout the piece. This introduction is followed by supporting explanations and details. The first chapter in the book should give a general picture of the book as a whole. The first paragraph in each section should say what that section is all about. And within each paragraph, the leading sentence should give the general gist of the paragraph, which is then supported by details or facts. It is also best, at the end of a book or section, to write a conclusion, reviewing the important ideas or reasoning in the book; and the same thing often helps at the end of a section, to summarize the key points in the section.

Transition. Good writers use transitions to link the end of each section to the next section. For example, at the end of a "Planning" section and before "Implementation," one might say, "When the planning phase is completed, the recommendations should be implemented without delay."

Focus. If you want your readers to get the main thrust of your work, omit side issues or tangents and focus on your principal ideas.

Brevity. Short words, sentences, and paragraphs usually make for easier reading. An exception is that common words should be used instead of uncommon words even if the common word is long. A paragraph of a half page or more looks like a dark, forbidding mass of words, so try to break it up into pieces. As an aid, the WordPerfect® word processing program will count the average number of words per sentence and the average word length. It can also identify several types of grammatical errors and suggest ways to correct them.

Audience. A good writer never forgets the audience. Use technical jargon only if it will be understood by those you expect to read the item. Make sure the terms you use will be readily comprehended by those with the education and experience levels of your readers.

Editing. Every word should carry its own weight. Adverbs and adjectives often can be deleted; they are subjective terms, whereas nouns and verbs are more concrete. Review each piece and cross off adjectives and adverbs that are not essential to the meaning. Your writing will become clearer and more understandable, as well as shorter.

Thinking. It has been said that "writing is thinking," meaning that the process of writing makes the author think ideas through. This is one reason the outline plays an important part in writing. When you have difficulty putting something into words, it is usually because you really haven't thought it through fully. When this occurs, ask yourself, "What am I really trying to say? Do I really understand the point I am trying to explain?" Asking these questions will usually rectify the writing block or obstacle.

Revision. After you have drafted a piece, it is usually beneficial to set it aside for a few days; then review it for clarity, logical arrangement, and accuracy. It is particularly important to check for any ambiguity; look at every sentence and ask if it is possible for the reader to get a meaning other than what you intended. Think "How can I make this part clearer? Or more logical?" Then rewrite those parts that can be improved.

Grammar. It can be damaging to a professional image to use improper grammar. If you are not sure of the rules, use a dictionary and a style book. If you are doing extensive book-length writing, it may be worth getting an editor's guidebook, like *The Chicago Manual of Style*, published by The University of Chicago Press.

Newsletters

Many consultants use newsletters to reinforce their reputations as experts in their specialties, to keep their names in front of prospective clients, and sometimes to add to their income. Newsletters are usually sent monthly, quarterly, or on some other regular schedule. Their content can be editorial, expressing viewpoints on issues in the field, or they can contain abstracts of articles, writings by other specialists, or even chatty or humorous items included to enhance the readers' interest.

Newsletters are normally printed on 11" x 17" paper which folds to the standard 8 1/2" x 11" size, and are typically four or eight pages long. The consultant's or firm's logo is prominently displayed, sometimes with a few words about the publisher. Many newsletters include two columns per page. Most word processing software can produce distinctive and professional looking copy. Desktop publishing software can provide additional special features.

Newsletters are sent to past and prospective clients and to other contacts who might send business your way. In other words, publishing a newsletter can be a key part of the merchandising process you use to build up your reputation and become known as an authority in your specialty.

Some newsletter publishers send newsletters out free, as a merchandising device. Others charge a subscription price. Some do both, with the free copies going to special friends and consulting prospects. Lists are developed from past clients, friends, association members, and other sources. You can develop one by going to the library and searching business directories for executives in specialties or industries, identified by their Standard Industrial

Classification code numbers. You could also create the list based on titles, such as Finance VP or Research VP, or based on geographical areas of interest. One good source is Dun & Bradstreet's *Million Dollar Directory* which is available at most libraries. You can also obtain lists, with similar selection criteria, through sellers of mailing lists. This is a lot easier, but it costs. For mailing list providers, check the yellow pages and the Internet.

If you want to get ideas by reviewing what newsletters other consultants have published, for $25 you can rent for a month a collection of actual examples, "Sample House Organs/Newsletters—Item No. M-1106-CN," from Kennedy Publications, Templeton Road, Fitzwilliam, New Hampshire 03447, (800) 531–9555.

Two pages of *Computer Security Digest*, a successful and informative newsletter which has been published for many years, appear on pages 66–67.

Computer Security Digest is prepared by G. Jack Bologna, JD, CFE, president of Computer Protection Systems, Inc., an organization providing counsel in computer security, audit, and control. He is the author of *Fraud Auditing and Forensic Accounting, Accountants' Handbook of Fraud and Commercial Crime,* and *Corporate Fraud.* Jack also is editor of the newsletter *Forensic Accounting Review*. He is an associate professor at Siena Heights College in Adrian, Michigan.

Jack mentioned that he finds editing his two newsletters helps him stay on top of important developments in his consulting specialties.

Speaking

Writing and speaking activities can feed on each other. If a speech is of interest to specialists in your field, then it is likely that an article on the same subject also would be appealing. Conversely, if readers appreciate an article, one of them may well say, "Let's get so-and-so to give a talk about it at our next monthly dinner meeting, or our annual conference." The preparation time for such a request is much less than preparing a new speech from scratch.

Some consultants find they can make writing and speaking the dominant part of their consulting business: for a few it's their exclusive business. This is especially true for consultants who have an unusual knack for speaking performances and writing books or regular columns in periodicals. However, most consultants get most of their revenue from problem-solving and advisory assignments. They use writing and speaking as supplements to their primary endeavors, with the knowledge that writing and speaking are effective tools for generat-

Computer Security Digest

Editor: Jack Bologna   ISSN. 0882 1453 Volume XIII, No. 12   March 1996

IN THIS ISSUE

I. NEWS BRIEFS

A. Internet Security Solutions Offered

1. The NCSA in Carlisle, PA., announced that it has established a program to test products from the 21 members of the Firewall Product Developers' Consortium. The NCSA will establish a baseline of capabilities that effective firewalls should offer. The group will certify for users which products meet those criteria.

   The association also will publish white papers to help users understand the issues they should consider when buying a firewall, said Peter Tippett, president of the NCSA.

   Tippett said the performance baseline for certification will be a list of security threats that rank high on three scales: likelihood of use by hackers, ease of use by hackers and amount of harm done by a successful attack. The idea is to develop a set of criteria that accounts for at least 90% of the risk and update the list as threats change, he said. (Computerworld, 2/5/96)

2. An Internet commerce company has written key elements of a software program that snatches credit-card numbers from on-line traffic. The firm wrote the program to demonstrate that securing on-line credit-card transactions may be impossible.

   Richard Quinter, director of information systems at FirstLine Trust Co., a Toronto finance firm, says that plucking credit-card numbers from the Internet "is the easiest thing in the world to do." He said when he was a computer science undergraduate, he and his classmates used software to steal one another's passwords and play pranks. (CW, 2/5/96)

Computer Protection Systems, Inc. 150 N. Main St., Plymouth, MI. 48170
Phone: (313) 459-8787 Fax (313) 459-2720

Computer Security Digest

3. "When organizations believe they will not be able to attain their operative goals, they often resort to illegal practices to reach them." (Perrow, 1961:855)

4. Departmentalization in larger organizations often creates operative goals for subunits that are different from the overall profitability goals of the organization. (Green, 1990:98)

5. Because specialization emphasizes subunit self-interest and diminishes external control and scrutiny, we can expect more crime in organizations that have more departmentalized structures. (Green, 1990:98)

ing the reputation and visibility so necessary to achieve their marketing goals.

This section will discuss ways to stimulate speaking requests, how to plan seminars, and helpful hints on how to strengthen your speaking skills.

How to Get Speaking Invitations

A principal method for securing speaking invitations is to volunteer to present a topic of interest at an upcoming meeting of a professional association, trade group, or business organization such as Kiwanis, Rotary, or Chambers of Commerce. You might also volunteer to speak to nonbusiness groups such as churches, schools, and community and civic organizations.

Business organizations are usually preferable because the audiences are more likely to be interested in your particular expertise. But giving talks to nonbusiness groups can help you practice making presentations, sharpen your speaking skills, and give you greater poise in front of an audience (though even very experienced speakers often feel tension before they start to talk). The nonbusiness groups may also be of important value to consultants who serve the general public, such as personal finance counselors or career advisors.

Organizations typically pay nothing or a modest honorarium, and possibly travel expenses, for a technical or business presentation. So talking before these groups is usually not worthwhile for the money alone. Its principal value to a consultant is the resulting publicity and recognition. The low pay is one reason not many people compete for these speaking platforms, and your likelihood of acceptance is favorable.

However, some prominent speakers who have attained outstanding reputations can command huge fees, especially at large gatherings. Some of the well-paid presenters are as much inspirational as informational.

Seminars

There are two quite different ways to provide seminars: arranging them entirely by yourself, or doing them for a fee for an organization in the business of running seminars.

Producing Your Own Seminars. When you promote and conduct your own seminars, there many time-consuming tasks that take a lot of work and some money. But the profits can be significant. The work is not difficult, but it can take considerable time. The promotion part involves creating the sales material, getting the mailing lists, and mailing the publicity documents. Then you must arrange for a location, after guessing the number of people who will attend. Someone must be on hand to greet the attendees, check their payment, and give them handouts. Visual aids should be prepared and the display equipment must be arranged for; most hotels and convention centers have presentation equipment available. You may want to have another presenter collaborate with you to give variety or cover a special part of the topic.

All this preparation makes for a significant investment, with a big unknown being the number who will attend. If it is a series of seminars, your initial experience will give you a closer approximation of the size of subsequent audiences.

Seminars can be a one-shot deal, or repeated at different venues or at different times in the same place, maybe every six months or year. Karl Schricker had a seminar business called Manuals Corporation of America, and had developed a reputation as the leading expert on how to prepare policy, procedure, and other manuals. A main part of his income was from two three-day seminars a year at which he had a few other speakers present different aspects of the subject to large audiences. Often he was asked to put on seminars for individual companies. The rest of the time he spent giving counsel to individual clients on the subject he knew so well.

Seminar Management Organizations. Having a seminar management enterprise retain you to conduct one or more of its seminars is much different than running the seminars yourself. All the time required for arranging and merchandising the seminar is their responsibility. So is the opportunity for a significant profit, or loss. Fees can range from modest to substantial, depending largely on the popularity of the speaker. Some consultants with topics of wide appeal make seminar presentations a major part of their consulting time and revenue.

Some seminar management organizations are listed in the table that follows:

Seminar Management Organizations

Alexander Hamilton Institute (908) 852–3699	605 Grand Avenue P.O. Box 794 Hacketstown, NJ 07840
American Management Association (800) 262–0699	P.O. Box 169 Saranac Lake, NY 12983
Center for Advanced Professional Development (714) 261–0240	1820 East Gary Street Suite 110 Santa Ana, CA 92705
National Seminars Group (800) 258–7246	6901 West 63d Street P.O. Box 2949 Shawnee Mission, KS 66201
MIS Training Institute (508) 879–7999	498 Concord Street Framingham, MA 01701
SkillPath Seminars (800) 873–7545	P.O. Box 2768 Mission, KS 66201

When you offer your services to such seminar providers, they will ask for your credentials and speaking experience. Some may also ask for a videotape of one of your prior presentations, which can be a helpful means of demonstrating your capability and effectiveness as a seminar presenter.

College and University Courses

Many consultants teach college and university courses as a supplement to their other consulting activities. Conducting these courses produces benefits similar to those of presenting seminars. But teaching has one advantage and one disadvantage.

The advantage is that being affiliated with a college or university yields a higher level of recognition than seminars do. Working for a college or university reinforces your image as an authority on whatever the subject may be. The disadvantage is that the course schedule requires a regular time obligation which may interfere with travel and other activities of your consulting practice.

Tips on Preparing and Giving Talks

The art of giving effective talks and presentations is one about which much has been written and discussed. It would be impossible to cover the field thoroughly here, but it may be helpful to review key points to strengthening presentation skills, making preparations, and conducting talks.

Developing Speaking Skills. Practice is helpful in developing ability and ease in giving talks and presentations. Speaking to association, business, social, or civic groups is one way to get that practice. If you are asked to be president or chair of such a group, you will be out in front and running meetings. If you are serious about developing speaking skills, you can get guidance and practice from instruction organizations like the Dale Carnegie Institute or others that may be listed under Public Speaking Instruction in the yellow pages. And you can join the National Speakers Association (5201 North 7th Street, Suite 200, Phoenix AZ 85014) and meet with others who have the same interests and objectives.

Making Preparations. After making the outline or notes for a talk, the next step is usually the preparation of visual aids and handouts. Audiences learn by seeing as well as by hearing, so having visual aids increases understanding, and helps keep the audience's interest as well. The visual aids can be simple, like a flip chart and pens, or transparencies, or your can use sophisticated computer-aided visuals. Most speakers make individual copies of their visual aids as handouts for the attendees. This enables the audience to keep the visual aids to jog their memories, and to take notes as the speaker moves through the outlined topics. Other handouts you can give to the audience include copies of articles on the same or related subjects, and a flyer about your consulting business.

Conducting the Talk. Whether it is a one-hour talk or an all-day presentation, your main objective is to develop and maintain the audience's interest. The hints listed next are techniques for overcoming the tendency for listeners to become bored and have their minds wander.

- Start with a bit of humor, which can arouse initial interest; and include other jokes from time to time.
- Get audience participation. You might ask listeners at the beginning about their experience on some aspect of the subject, then get them to volunteer their ideas or practices on a particular issue during the talk. Encouraging questions during the presen-

tation can also help the audience take an active role, though some presenters prefer not to be distracted from their exposition steps and would rather ask for questions at the end.

- Always speak extemporaneously. Never read from prepared text. Most effective speakers put their key thoughts on cards or on a written outline as their reference guide. Some project their outline on a screen and use it as a visual aid.

- Practice your delivery. Talking with enthusiasm, using inflections, and moving around are ways to bolster attention. Practicing and rehearsing the talk in advance can help solidify in your mind the sequence of the points to make, and sometimes help you develop effective wording. It can also make you more relaxed when giving the presentation.

Setting up a Seminar

Planning a seminar involves selecting the venue, arranging for a receptionist to greet the attendees, preparing badges, handouts and any products to be sold, then checking in advance to make sure the visual aids and other arrangements are ready.

The most usual places to hold a seminar are hotels or social and athletic clubs, although other places may be suitable. The person who greets the arrivals should be pleasant and businesslike, and should give the attendees their badges, if any, and handouts, which generally should include flyers about the presenter, copies of relevant articles the presenter (or some other author) has written, and an outline or other summary of the seminar. If the presenter has written books or produced video or audio cassettes on topics related to the talk, the receptionist can help promote and sell those products.

If the seminar is a half-day or full day, the morning and afternoon sessions should be no more than three or four hours long, with at least one break of about 15 minutes scheduled at about the middle of each morning and afternoon session.

By-Products and Services

Cassettes are natural by-products of the writing and speaking independent consultants do. There are other types of products that are also natural adjuncts to consulting activities such as providing training, a service, or computer hardware and software.

Videocassettes

Videocassettes can be by-products of speaking activities, either seminars or separate speaking engagements. You can create a videocassette recording rather easily by arranging to tape one of your seminars or presentations. These cassettes can then be produced and packaged by a business that specializes in that service. You can then sell these tapes at subsequent seminars and presentations, as well by mailing merchandising flyers to lists of persons who may be interested in the product.

Audiotapes

Larry Bassett, whose consulting business is described in Appendix A, routinely tapes his many talks and presentations by putting a microcassette recorder in his pocket with the microphone attached to his lapel. He then offers to sell copies of those tapes to members of the audience and others. Sometimes Larry will give one of the tapes to a potential client as part of his marketing activities.

Other Products and Services

Consultants can offer many other types of products and services that fit in well with their regular consulting activities. Two examples are training and computer hardware and software.

Many consultants provide training as a side line, and a few consultants make training a major part of the assistance they offer clients. It is natural for an organization desiring training for a group of employees—sales staff, customer service representatives, or computer programmers—to engage a consultant to conduct the training sessions. When the consultant is an authority in any function such as these and has skills in training, using the consultant's services to educate and motivate a specialized group of employees is an effective way for clients to achieve their training goals. A consultant is often the best choice as a trainer because the training time is limited and doesn't warrant hiring an employee. Also, the consultant is an outside authority on the subject and may command more respect.

Selling computer hardware or software can be a logical related activity for a consultant whose primary service is developing and installing computer systems. Some firms whose primary activity is selling computer hardware and software also sell related consulting services. These arrangements can benefit clients who are interested in results and are pleased to have one person or firm accountable for those results.

There is a potential conflict of interest in these arrangements, however, because an unethical consultant might push a more costly product than is necessary to gain greater profit. It is important that the clients be aware in these cases that the sale of the product is a profit-making part of the consultant's activities.

Checklist　The following checklist will help you review the issues in this chapter and consider these matters in your consulting plans or practice.

	Yes	No
Have you written articles for publication?		
Have you written books for publication?		
Have your publications produced client leads?		
Have you contacted periodical editors about writing articles on your ideas or successful accomplishments?		
Do you make and review outlines before preparing a speech or article?		
Do your writings have lots of headings?		
Do you make introductory summaries before each part you write or speak?		
Do you use short words, sentences, and paragraphs?		
Do you avoid adjectives and adverbs?		
Do you review and revise your writing carefully for clarity and grammar?		
Do you use newsletters as a marketing or revenue-producing device?		
Do you consider writing articles on the topics of your speeches?		
Do you volunteer to make presentations?		
Are seminars a part of the services you offer?		
Have you practiced speaking skills?		
Do you encourage audience participation at your talks?		
Have you considered videocassettes or audio cassettes as supplementary income sources?		

How to Market Your Firm's Services

For most independent consultants, marketing is the main key to success. Chapter 2 discussed how to get started, hopefully achieving a few engagements in the first year. But 90 percent of consultants fail in the first two years. Some of these failures may represent displaced persons who pursued consulting more out of need than desire. But most consulting business declines are due to the failure to do the right kind of marketing, or enough marketing, to develop a stream of new engagements and clients. Too often, making a full effort on the first job, without taking time out to do marketing, leaves the new consultant high and dry when that initial assignment is completed.

One reason that marketing is difficult for independent consulting businesses is that marketing involves a considerable lead time between the effort put out and the clients and engagements coming in. Good marketing involves taking time to become widely known and respected through many avenues, such as association activities, writing, and speaking. Some new consultants have the advantage of an established reputation in their specialties. Most, however, are competent and skilled, but not sufficiently well known to be asked frequently to perform or bid on consulting projects.

A relationship of trust must usually be developed between consultant and client, and that too takes time, often requiring several meetings.

Another way for an independent consultant to secure business is through one or more intermediary agencies. There are many brokers, membership groups, and organizations making temporary executive placements that perform these intermediary services. They find jobs or leads for consultants with various types of fee arrangements. We will review these business sources and explain how to find them, how likely they are to succeed, and how to deal with them.

Consultants who seek individuals as clients rather than organizations can use other ways also to generate consulting business. Their developing of referrals through contacts is usually an important client source which can be supplemented by various mail, phone, and advertising promotional efforts.

Referrals and Networking

Referrals developed over time through networking are a principal source of new clients and engagements for most independent consultants performing problem-solving and advisory services. Networking is developing a wide range of contacts who know you and your work and are willing to refer clients to you. When an acquaintance tells these contacts about a problem, these contacts will say, "I know a consultant who has just the experience you need, and who does fine work." You create such contacts by being active in associations and social groups, writing and speaking, keeping in touch personally, and through other related tactics.

Networking, of course, should be a process with mutual benefits. The conscious or unconscious motivation of others meeting with you is to gain something of value from you, such as a tip to help them in their jobs or a lead on someone else who might assist them. Sometimes as mutual benefits result from a contact, a relationship will progress from business contact to acquaintance and even sometimes to friend. As a bond strengthens, the relationship increases in value to all concerned.

Associations and Other Groups

Participating in groups like professional and trade associations is one of the best ways to develop helpful contacts. Attending such groups' affairs is useful as they usually include socializing that can help you make acquaintances in your particular profession and exchange information on your business activities and interests.

Actively participating in such groups can lead to even stronger relationships. If you accept positions such as a committee chair or officer, you have a chance to become more closely connected with the people you work with. Most organizations are delighted for people to volunteer for such roles. When you do perform some leadership activity, your peers get to know you more fully and, if you do a good job, know firsthand your competence and reliability, which they can attest to in speaking to others. Such activities take time and pay nothing, so you must regard them as marketing activity with a by-product benefit of keeping up-to-date in your professional specialty.

Another advantage to association participation is that it can often lead to being asked to speak at a luncheon or dinner meeting, which will further reinforce your reputation as an authority in your field and make you known and respected by your audience.

The associations can be of two types: (1) consultant groups, and (2) groups in your specialty, which may be engineering, human relations, materials handling, or whatever. Members of consultant groups may be your competitors, but since consultants vary their specialties, there is often a give and take. I may be helping a client with a cost reduction project who also is interested in an executive compensation analysis, which is your specialty. So I might ask you if you are interested. This type of lead is what marketing efforts attempt to generate.

Nontechnical associations are better for consultants who serve the general public, such as investment advisors or bridal consultants. Such consultants would do best to circulate among civic groups, social and religious groups, and organizations like Kiwanis or Rotary.

Speaking and Writing

Speaking can be an excellent means of making contacts who may be able to say a good word, suggest a lead, or even offer to be a client. Such speaking can be in a wide variety of situations: at local association meetings or national conferences, seminars created by you or by a commercial training organization, college and university classes, or other gatherings.

At these sessions, take advantage of every opportunity to meet people personally. Circulate before and after the presentations, ask people you meet about their businesses, inquire diplomatically as to any special problems they may have, offer general advice on any matters they ask about, and collect the business cards of potential clients and other worthwhile contacts. Those business cards can be used for two purposes later on: (1) to phone the individuals to show an interest and listen for clues about problems that might be the basis for an engagement, and (2) to put into a database of contact persons to whom you will send articles of interest, maybe your newsletter, or other promotional material.

Writing does not produce valuable contacts as directly as speaking engagements. However, writing can stimulate invitations to speak, and it helps in that way. And, if people in your audience have seen things you have written, that may encourage them to want to meet you after the session and ask you about issues discussed in your articles or books. Also, copies of an article you have written can be a useful marketing tool when given to a prospective client who may be interested in engaging you on a matter related to the article's topic.

Other Related Approaches

Amy Steven's article, "Use Your Kids, and Other Tips for Hungry Lawyers" (November 27, 1995, *The Wall Street Journal*) describes several marketing strategies for attorneys. Individual attorneys, like individual consultants, rely on networking as a primary means of securing clients, so most of the thoughts in this article are sound advice for consultants, too. The article applies especially to consultants whose clients are individuals. The recommendations suggest a more aggressive approach than many consultants might feel comfortable with. However, the point is well made that it is wise to take advantage of every possible type of personal contact as a potential way to promote your business. A particularly good point is this marketing specialist's emphasis on keeping notes about your contacts—such as their spouses, kids, and hobbies—as a way to later make conversation on matters of interest and importance to them.

A summary of that *Wall Street Journal* article, which appeared in the paper's "Lawyers and Clients" section, is shown next.

Highlights of

"Use Your Kids, and Other Tips for Hungry Lawyers"

by Amy Stevens

This article in *The Wall Street Journal* of November 27, 1995, reported on methods recommended for lawyers to use in day-to-day contacts to develop clients and market their services. It includes the ideas and experiences of Vera Sullivan, who conducts seminars for lawyers on how to obtain clients and business, and of four other marketing consultants who advise attorneys on their sales strategies.

Sullivan's theme is that lawyers should actively promote their business rather than passively waiting for clients. A main tenet of hers is "Think of every social encounter as an opportunity to do business." Social encounters take place while coming out of church, going to exercise groups, waiting in theater lines, and attending children's school activities.

The article mentions that many attorneys feel uncomfortable with aggressive marketing tactics. It also quotes Sol M. Linowitz, a distinguished attorney, statesman, and book author who criticizes the constant passing out of business cards, and who, speaking of the old days, said, "We had a sense of dignity and we were proud of that."

The article cites six suggested activities for marketing legal services. Ms. Sullivan advises lawyers to select the approaches that will produce the best return for the time spent.

1. At the Gym

People who go to health clubs have abundant opportunities to start conversations and make acquaintances. Ms. Sullivan recommends devising ways to bring business cards to these places and passing them out when appropriate. She suggests starting up conversations by using small talk or asking questions about issues of the day.

2. Use Your Kids

Ms. Sullivan suggests strategies such as offering to give a talk at a local school or becoming a coach for a children's soccer team. One of her clients met the parent of another member of his child's soccer team when rooting for the team. That acquaintance became a client. Ms. Sullivan's attorney client said he was surprised to discover that his kid's soccer game might be a place where he could develop some business.

3. Send Cards and Gifts

Three different legal marketing consultants offered suggestions in this category. One recommends sending a card or gift to prospects who do not return phone calls, as a means of visibly reminding them of your presence. His clients have sent whitewater rafting books, juggling balls, and bonsai kits to client prospects. A second consultant recommends sending holiday cards on recycled paper to demonstrate your civic and social concerns. The third consultant counsels attorneys to mail three handwritten memos each week, using occasions like birthdays and memorial services as the reason.

Incidentally, the five marketing consultants referred to in this article, who specialize in advising lawyers, indicate a remarkable potential niche for this type of consulting service. The fees of the marketing consultants interviewed in the article are quite substantial. One consultant obtains up to $15,000 for audiences of 25 at two sessions.

continued

---

4. Go Dancing

One of Ms. Sullivan's clients took her suggestion for helping to establish a practice specializing in senior citizens. The 29-year-old attorney goes once a month to a dance for the elderly. He reported one beneficial result: a woman who asked him to represent her in a case of age discrimination, which he won for her.

5. Make Contacts during Plane Travel

A bankruptcy lawyer took the advice of one of the marketing counselors and reported favorable results. He had previously regularly used plane travel time for reading. His advisor suggested he try to develop contacts during these periods. Then, during a trip he noticed a lady in first class using a cellular phone, and he figured she might be an executive. He starting by making some small talk, and the conversation ended with his obtaining an additional client.

6. Keep Notes on Your Contacts

A Detroit marketing consultant recommends taking and maintaining notes about your contacts: their children, interests, vacations, ideas, hobbies, family names—"down to the tiniest details." She suggests writing down these notes soon after the meeting while they are fresh in your mind. You can keep them on paper, file cards, or in computer files. When you next meet and can ask about clients' spouses or children by name, it shows your interest in them as people and in the things that matter to them.

Keep in Touch   Keep the contacts you develop by networking warm. Talk with them by phone periodically, send items of interest as a favor, and otherwise repeatedly make them aware of your presence, talents, and availability.

You can phone clients to discuss a new development in an area of mutual interest, or to inquire how a matter they have discussed before is coming along. You don't want to be a pest, so keep an ear open for their responding favorably to the call, or possibly being under pressure and wanting to make it short.

You might mail a contact a copy of an article regarding a matter that person is worrying about, maybe with a handwritten note that says, "John, thought this might be of interest. Regards, Bill." If you prepare newsletters, these are a fine way of keeping your business in view of former and potential clients and other contacts. Of, if you have broadened into a new subspecialty, and you want to let people in your database know about that, send them a new brochure or flyer with a personally addressed cover letter.

All networking contacts belong in a database, hopefully on your computer, or at least on a Rolodex. Keep a log of your contacts, and notes about the individuals' interests, background, and personal lives. These are all important to fostering stronger relationships with business contacts by showing an interest in their business and personal matters, over time.

Brochures and Flyers

Brochures are a frequently used publicity item and generally describe the consultant's or firm's specialties and services, its modus operandi, credentials, and possibly types or names of clients served.

Often these brochures are on 8 1/2" by 11" paper, folded in thirds to fit into standard #10 envelopes. You may attach them to proposals to go on record as to the essentials about your firm, or you may hand one to a contact who asks for it or who requests information about your consulting business.

Some consultants develop more elaborate brochures, say 8 1/2" by 11" folders of four to eight pages, explaining in some detail the services they provide. These may include a few examples of engagements and their beneficial results, and a lengthy list of clients served.

Quite a few consultants operate without a brochure. One has said that if a prospective client wants to know more about him, he provide a few articles he has written, and doing so usually suffices.

One good brochure example is the one shown next of Robert B. Fast, one of the successful consultants described in some detail in Appendix A. This four-page folder fits into a #10 envelope.

PRODUCT/PROCESS

Bob Fast, president of Robert B. Fast Associates, Inc., spent his entire working life in research in the food industry. He is a product development person with a flair for process development and production problem-solving.

Procass Equipment Selection

The four product and process patents Bob has in the snack and cereal field prove his ability to pick the right equipment for the right job.

Production Problem Solving

He is an expert in spotting production bottlenecks and developing creative solutions to knotty problems.

PROFESSIONAL

Inside

DEVELOPMENT

Product Development

Bob's thirty years' experience in product development covered areas of milling and baking, cereal processing, snack food development, pet food processing and many more.

Project Administration

Every project has many bases to be touched to reach a successful goal: development, equipment selection and testing, shelf-life testing, organoleptic testing, packaging and shipping testing—all must be managed into an integrated plan and timetable. Having done it, we have the expertise to see that it is done correctly for you.

Supplier Contact Assistance

Thirty years of product and process development experience has created a voluminous file of supplier contacts for equipment and products of all kinds for the food industry.

Organoleptic and Analytical Laboratory Assistance

Quality control and assurance are a MUST for every food product and process. Assistance can be rendered in setting up lab tests or finding outside labs to perform needed work.

PROVEN

Situated in the southwest corner of Vermont, Poultney is within easy access of all major airlines.

BURLINGTON, VT
Int'l. Airport

1½ HRS.

POULTNEY, VT   ½ HR.   RUTLAND, VT
★   Regional
                          Airport

1½ HRS.   1 HR.

              4 HRS.

ALBANY, NY   Logan Int'l.
Airport   Airport
                          BOSTON, MA

LET US HELP YOU

Call or Write Today

RD #2 Box 404
Poultney, VT 05764
802-287-9516

Back

Bob Fast, Pres.

CONTSULTANTS TO THE FOOD INDUSTRY

SERVICES AVAILABLE

- PRODUCT DEVELOPMENT
- PRODUCTION PROBLEM SOLVING
- PROCESS EQUIPMENT SELECTION
- SUPPLIER CONTACT ASSISTANCE
- PROJECT ADMINISTRATION
- ORGANOLEPTIC & ANALYTICAL LABORATORY ASSISTANCE

RD #2 Box 404
Poultney, VT 05764
802-287-9516

Front

The following hypothetical brochure is made on 8 1/2" x 11" paper folded into thirds.

PRINCIPAL SPECIALTIES
AND SERVICES

- methods engineering of administrative practices
- organization analysis and strungthening
- management audits
- policy and procedure manuals and documentation
- cost reduction programs
- work simplification and measurement
- computer studies and applications
- computer security
- financial planning and controls
- records management
- executive search

TYPES OF BUSINESSES SERVED

- banking
- insurance
- retail
- wholesale
- transportation
- manufacturing
- nonprofit organizations
- government agencies

These include centralized and divisionalized companies with sales from $ 10 million to $ 12 billion.

CONSULTING
APPROACH

A preliminary survey will outline what improvements and results we can expect to accomplish for your organization.

The imporvment program will then be designed and conducted to meet your particular needs and objectives and adapted to your circumstances and business environment.

During the study, you will receive periodic reports of the progress made and remaining actions planned.

We regard each assignment as a personal service to the individual who retains us. Therefore, we assure that the client first becomes acquainted with the person who will do the assignment, and that a sound mutual understanding and relationship are well established in advance. That includes a clear definition of the consulting goals and expectations.

Inside

**Robert A. Jones
Associates**

*Management Consulting
Services*

200 East Fairway Drive
Ajax Township, NM 22222

(999) 888-7777
Fax:
(999) 888-7778

Front

Robert A. Jones

Background

Served many corporations for 30 years in a wide range of management engineering areas including organization, policies, and procedures... management information systems... documentation... organizing and managing systems and procedures department functions.

Directed research on management techniques for the Society of Systems management and the Financial Executives Council.

Credentials

CMC - Certified Management Consultant
CSP - Certified Systems Professional

Publications

Manuals Management
Computer Planning Handbook

Back

News Releases

News releases can serve as an effective means for inexpensively gaining recognition, particularly to publicize some event or change that will interest readers of trade periodicals, newspapers, or newsletters in your field.

The news release is relatively easy to prepare and distribute at very little cost. It involves preparing a one- or two-page document and looking up the editors of publications whose readers would find the news item of interest. The publications' editors like news releases because it is easy for them to convert releases into brief items in their publications without having to pay an author to do research.

Announcements that lend themselves to news releases are matters of value to the publication's readers. Such topics might be the formation of a new consulting firm in a needed specialty, establishment of a branch office of a consulting firm, development of a valuable new technique, or the publication of a book on an innovative approach.

Follow these rules to make your news release effective and acceptable to the editors:

- Identify the paper as a release by typing the words *News Release, News,* or *Release* at the top of the first page.
- Double-space the copy, and print one side only.
- Include your or your firm's name prominently.
- Give the name and phone number of a person to call if there is any question.
- Type ###, End, or -30- at the end of the release.
- State near the top *For Immediate Release,* or *For Release on (date).*
- Limit text to two pages.

For a sample news release incorporating the above principles, see the next page.

Mail Marketing

There are a variety of ways to use the mail as part of a merchandising program. Mass mailings are sometimes helpful. Some types of mailings directed at specific potential clients can be effective. Newsletters, when well done, are usually a strong drawing card. All of these mail approaches require a well-developed and carefully maintained address database.

Mass Mailings

Sending out brochures describing your services to a list of potential clients can help make them aware of your skills and your availability. But sending out flyers alone seldom

Robert A. Jones Associates
200 East Fairway Drive
Ajax Township, NM 22222

NEWS RELEASE

For further information call: ***For Immediate Release***
Robert A. Jones
(999) 888-7777

NEW COST REDUCTION PROCESS DEVELOPED
ELIMINATING USUAL PAIN

The Robert A. Jones Associates has developed a **PAINLESS COST
REDUCTION** process that enables companies to cut their operating costs
without the resentments, disruption, and confusion that usually accompany
such cost savings programs. This new method has been developed and
refined in the conduct of four recent client programs in which the
companies served have cut cost between 5% and 30% in some departments
without the drawbacks that occur when other methods have been applied.

Robert A. Jones Associates is a consulting firm with four associates which
has operated in New Mexico and in southern California for 12 years, in areas
of methods engineering, organization analysis and strengthening, and work
simplification and measurement.

The **PAINLESS COST REDUCTION** methodology has been created by
combining special human relations as well as methods engineering
principles.

###

brings significant responses. It is better to send a letter or notice about some new development that may stimulate interest, possibly with your flyer attached.

If the mailing results in inquiries, you can follow up to explore the possibilities of a consulting engagement. If there is no immediate interest or need for your services, those responders still should be added to your database of potential clients and sent subsequent mailings.

In any mass mailing it is a sound marketing strategy to ask for some response. Achieving a response identifies those people who have at least a fleeting interest in your consulting services. Phone respondents to explore further the nature of their interest, and add respondents to your database as potential clients.

One mechanism for generating responses is to send out questionnaires and offer to mail the respondents copies of the report based on the questionnaire replies. Those questionnaires can be worded to provide clues about respondents' potential interest in your consulting services.

Specialized Mailings

One effective type of mailing targets executives who have recently moved to new positions, either within their present organizations or at new companies. In either case they have taken on new, often higher, executive responsibilities. These executives' new responsibilities often make them uncertain about their new environments and willing to chat with an outsider who is knowledgeable about the areas in which they may have some questions.

Two prime sources of daily information about top executives changing positions are *The Wall Street Journal* and *The New York Times.*

The idea is to send memos to relocated executives giving them a general picture of your capabilities and offering to meet with them to discuss any matters in your field that may interest them. It usually takes time and several phone calls to arrange such a meeting, and you may succeed only 10 to 20 percent of the time. But when you can arrange a meeting, it presents an opportunity to find out what is of concern to executives in their new positions.

The first meeting is usually to get acquainted and start building a feeling of trust. Usually a first meeting will end with your promise to give the issues more thought and schedule a second meeting soon to talk about specifics. At an appropriate time, you can suggest creating a brief survey to give the executive your objective, independent, and knowledgeable judgment on the issues discussed.

Before the first meeting you should research the client's company and the client. That will enable you to show more than a casual interest, and to easily start off with small talk about such matters as recent acquisitions mergers, or a good profit report. If clients are listed in *Who's Who*, you can research their college, writings, clubs, family, prior positions, and so on.

This process takes time, but it is one effective way of developing a strong relationship and a possible assignment, which can then grow into a larger engagement or several projects.

A sample letter aimed at new executives appears on page 88. Most consultants would also enclose a brochure summarizing their credentials and accomplishments.

Experience indicates that about one in five or ten of such letters may result in a meeting, and one of every two or three persons met with can result in an engagement.

In the meetings it is helpful to ask a lot of questions about the company and the interviewee, based on the research you prepared in advance. Depending on how the conversation progresses, you can inquire about how the new position is coming, changes they hope to make, and obstacles or difficulties they expect to face. Then, of course, you should discuss further any of the potential client's responses that may indicate areas where a consulting service might be beneficial. Hopefully, you may be able to say something like, "One of my clients had a very similar problem, and this is what we were able to accomplish for them."

One disadvantage to this method of finding consulting prospects is that some may meet with you only to "pick your brains," or even just to pass the time of day. That is a chance you must take in your many efforts to secure new clients. If their negative purpose is apparent, of course, drop the prospect. But often it is not easy to evaluate prospective clients, and a hesitant initial interest sometimes turns into a strong positive one later.

Copies of Articles

The point of maintaining a list of interested contacts is to keep them aware of your capabilities and potential value. One way to do this is by sending them copies of articles they might enjoy. Articles you have authored are best, but it is also fine to send writings of others that may interest your contacts.

Contacts, of course, are your prospect database. Contacts include current clients, former clients, prospective clients, and anyone you know who might be in a position to refer possible clients to you.

COMPUTER SECURITY ASSOCIATES
22222 Twenty Second Street
Navaho, Arizona 33333
(555) 444–3333

Name of Finance Vice President
Company Name
Street
City, State, Zip

Dear Mr./Ms. Finance Vice President:

Our firm designed a security plan which enabled a 200-member brokerage office to operate normally in one business day after the World Trade Center disaster.

Most top corporate officers have security concerns when they think about other recent events, such as:

The 5,000 automated teller machines shut down from a roof collapsed by snow.

The San Francisco earthquake, which disabled 50 major firms for over a week.

The 300 firms shut down by floods from a water main break in Chicago.

The attached folder describes Computer Security Associates' experience and capabilities in providing protective measures against such potential calamities.

I will phone you in a few days about a brief meeting in which we might discuss these matters.

Sincerely yours,

Robert R. Roberts
President

If the list is large, you can send articles with a form cover letter individually addressed. In cases where there is a more personal relationship, or where an article may be of special interest to the recipient, a friendly handwritten note would be preferable to a typed transmittal.

Newsletters

Newsletters have been discussed earlier as a possible revenue-producing product as well as a marketing device. The topic is mentioned again here only to remind readers that newsletters are one of the important methods of gaining continuous recognition as an authority in your consulting specialty, and they work even when you don't charge for them.

Another way to use newsletters as a phase of your marketing program is to send editorial or interesting factual items to other publishers of newsletters in your field. Most newsletter publishers are delighted to receive such material and are glad to print it, partly because as their deadlines approach, they may be happy to find material to fill up their newsletter pages.

Mail Sources, Databases

A main part of any marketing program for an independent consultant is a good record of prospects and referral contacts. The bare minimum is a Rolodex file. With today's computers, a database has become almost essential, as you can readily update, sort by criteria you select, and annotate with business and personal facts about each individual which are useful in refreshing your memory for future meetings with these individuals.

You can also code your database for use in different mailings. You might include codes for past clients, prospective clients, contacts in associations and business clubs, competitors who might be collaborators on projects, seminar attendees, newsletter recipients, and so on.

Sometimes lists purchased from mail list services may be worthwhile for distributing a promotional piece, such as sending out seminar advertisements to certain industries in specified geographical areas.

To Government Clients

Marketing consulting services to government agencies requires quite different procedures than marketing to commercial and other nonprofit organizations. The principal difference is that there are laws and regulations which require competitive bidding on consulting and other products and services purchased by federal, state, and local government agencies. These government procurement rules provide for dissemination of requests for proposals (RFPs) to potential providers of the products and services required. The proposals received are then opened and reviewed for conformity to the RFP's requirements, and awarded to the lowest bidder, or evaluated as to their qualitative worth and awarded to the lowest bidder among the proposals judged to be the best few.

These laws and regulations are designed to assure competition and fairness in selecting the proposal that best meets the requesting agency's objectives. The problems for the consultant are the considerable work necessary to meet the bureaucratic requirements, and the statistical odds of winning a proposal, which are one divided by the number of proposals submitted, which can be considerable.

However, some consultants learn the ropes and become skilled at beating the statistical odds of success. One such consultant is Herman Holtz, whose book *How to Succeed as an Independent Consultant* describes his techniques for securing government consulting contracts.

Two steps are necessary to be successful: (1) getting to know promptly of RFPs that may interest you, and (2) making your proposals selling documents as well as providing exactly the details required by the RFP.

One way to receive RFPs of interest is to secure an Application for Bidders List, Form 129, and send it to federal agencies that could have assignments within your specialties. These agencies will then send you RFPs for projects you might want to consider.

Commerce Business Daily (CBD) also lists items government agencies are interested in procuring, including consulting services. You can subscribe, or access CBD on a commercial database such as CompuServe. Contact state or local government agencies that might need your type of service by phone, by mail, or even in person, letting them know of your services and your desire to be informed of bidding opportunities.

If you are interested in pursuing a federal consulting business, become familiar with the Federal Acquisition Streamlining Act of 1994 which made some provisions to simplify smaller contracts, to arrange for agencies to work together in purchases of common interest, and to make other refinements in the federal procurement administration process.

Get into Directories

There are at least three directories of consultants and consulting firms which can be a source of inquiries from potential clients. Some organizations that need consulting assistance will use one of these directories to find firms that specialize in the help they require. Those potential clients then contact the consultants who seem likely prospects and ask for more information or possibly a proposal.

While inquiries from directory sources are certainly not a major source of business, it is easy and worthwhile to have yourself or your firm listed. These three directories describe briefly the consultant's or firm's scope and specialties, and they also cross-reference by functional and industrial categories. The three directories are:

The Directory of Management Consultants, 1995–1996, Fitzwilliam, NH: Kennedy Publications, 1995. (800) 531-0007.

Consulting and Consulting Organizations Directory, 15th edition, Detroit, MI: Gale Research Inc., 1994. (800) 347-4253.

Dun's Consultants Directory, 1996, Parsippany, NJ: Dun & Bradstreet, Inc., 1995. (800) 526-0651.

Research Potential Clients

Before meeting with a prospective client to discuss or negotiate a possible engagement, do some research to find out important facts about the company and recent events that are known in the public domain. Such facts include recent financial results, which are available from Dun & Bradstreet's *Million Dollar Directory*, and in other reference books readily available in any library or on computer commercial database services such as America Online, or on the Internet. Hoover's Online (http://www.hoovers.com/) has a database of 9,300 leading companies and can lead you to other related data sources. These sources also should give you a picture of the company's organization, products, and geographical locations.

Then check all references in the last year or two in such publications as *The Wall Street Journal* and *Business Week* to find out about labor issues, acquisitions, mergers, new products, legal questions, and other such matters that have been newsworthy. These findings may or may not have a bearing on the subject of your hoped for assignment, but they are helpful in early discussions to show your interest in the potential client's organization and to start clients talking about matters that interest them.

It is also beneficial to research the people with whom you hope to do business. If you can learn about that person's hobbies, colleges, family, or publications, those facts can help you make small talk and show your interest in a client. If the person is listed in *Who's Who*, which is available in most libraries, you can get a wealth of such details about the individual. Or you can use a library's database to find all the books that person has written.

These bits of personal information can be useful in developing a sound relationship with a client or potential client, which is one of the most important assets a consultant can have. Clients seldom contract for important consulting engagements unless they trust the consultant. This sense of trust, and the bond it can help strengthen, usually can be fostered over time through development of mutual respect and interests. It cannot be attained in a brief, stiff meeting discussing only the business issues at hand. Most satisfying business relationships include the added elements of friendship and trust reinforced by mutual interests and understanding.

Advertisements

Placing ads in newspapers, magazines, technical journals, or on TV or radio, is a technique most consultants generally don't use.

A few specialized periodicals have a page or two of ads for consultants in the field. These are relatively inexpensive, and may be worthwhile.

One consultant specializing in computer systems design tried a variety of advertisements over a three-year period just to test their effectiveness. He got no consulting work as a result of these ads, but he did receive a number of inquiries from people looking for jobs or selling computer equipment.

Advertising often is more worthwhile for consultants whose potential clientele is the general public in a specific area or region. These consultants could be personal financial advisors or career counselors. Placing appropriate ads for such services in local newspapers and periodicals is certainly appropriate and may well be worth their cost in the long run.

Phone Marketing

Cold marketing calls are suitable for many products and services, but generally are not effective with the more usual types of consulting. First, it is difficult and time-consuming to get to talk with decision makers. Calling to inquire about an executive's need for your service and trying to arrange a meeting is unlikely to produce consulting projects.

Making such calls might be effective if the call were preceded by a letter about a week earlier. The letter followed by a call would be something like the approach discussed earlier in Specialized Mailings. That approach is preferable because of the more likely interest from executives who have recently changed jobs, as described in that section.

However, phone calls to important contacts are an essential part of any independent consultant's marketing program. It is wise to think of good reasons to make such calls and to schedule them on your calendar, or in whatever reminder system you may have. Good reasons to call include such things as following up on how a suggestion you made earlier is working out, or asking if a person might want to sit with you on a flight to an upcoming conference.

Brokers and Referral Agencies

The marketing approaches and techniques reviewed earlier in this chapter, and also in the next, cover methods for securing consulting clients and engagements on your own. However, some consultants prefer to have others perform marketing services for them, for a fee, so they can then spend more of their time consulting and less time merchandising their services.

Many agencies and intermediaries can assist you in securing consulting clients or leads, and their services have become a profitable and growing business activity. These intermediary reference sources also are often used by consultants who do most of their marketing directly, but supplement the client engagements they secure themselves with references from referral agencies. These extra leads can provide additional work or help fill in gaps in your schedule.

Information Sources, and How to Use Them

Most of the information and concepts in the next sections have been taken from two sources, which are the results of extensive research and analysis of consulting referral and related agencies. These two books are:

Marketing and Matchmaking Services for Management Consultants, 63 pages, 1995, and

The Directory of Executive Temporary Placement Firms, 8th edition, 1995, 318 pages.

Both books are authored by Alice Snell and published by Kennedy Publications, Tempelton Road, Fitzwilliam, NH 03447.

The first book, *Marketing and Matchmaking Services for Management Consultants*, covers these categories:

Brokering services

Referral registries

Internet databases

Membership networks

Seminar facilitators

Consultant classes

It also discusses principal consulting associations, which are reviewed in the next chapter.

The second book, *The Directory of Executive Temporary Placement Firms*, covers firms which arrange temporary employment for executives. These are not consulting arrangements as such, but they may interest some independent consultants because of their limited duration and relatively high-level positions.

Each book has a page on each agency, describing the types of services they provide, specialties and industries covered, and, in many cases, with cogent comments about their values and limitations. For any management or other consultant interested in using the referral services of outside agencies, there is no better source than these two publications because they are based on thorough and professional research.

Kennedy Publications was started 25 years ago by James H. Kennedy with his newsletter *Consultant News*, which continues to offer information and advice for consultants. His Consultants Bookstore has an abundance of publications for consultants and clients, and many of its catalog's pithy comments are included in this book's bibliography. Mr. Kennedy has become an outstanding and influential leader in the consulting arena. His extensive publications and speeches offer insightful comments and cogent advice to consultants, consulting firms, and the associations which serve them.

Although the agencies described in this chapter provide the services they advertise, it is hard to judge in advance whether your odds of success are worth the cost. Most appear quite professional but caution always is indicated for firms that are new, and also for firms that charge twice by requesting a membership fee and a percent of the revenue you receive from clients.

Executive Temporary Placement Firms

The 8th edition of *The Directory of Executive Temporary Placement Firms* gives one-page summaries of the scope and methods of over 225 of these placement firms. The large number of these firms indicates the importance and growth of this phase of the placement industry. The downsizing trend has increased both the supply and demand sides of this business.

It is obviously quite profitable for these placement firms. They find it relatively easy to find candidates for their clients, though competition for clients is intense. Of course, no placement candidate is assured of finding even a temporary paying position.

Consulting or Not? Temporary executive positions are really not consulting engagements, but the two have much in common. They both require special experience and skills. The work of each is by definition temporary.

The difference is that clients looking for temporary executives usually want operating management types, people to run things. Consultants usually don't do hands-on work; they analyze problems, give advice, then leave, though many clients involve the consultant in the implementation phase.

In one sense, executive temporary placement firms compete with consultants. For example, if a company wants experienced people to develop a marketing plan for a new product in four months, it might be cheapest to hire temp executives at something near their former salaries. Consultants bill at double or several times their salary rate to cover marketing expenses, overhead, and profit.

Value to Consultants. Executive temporary placement may appeal to a displaced person who hasn't found another permanent job, has looked for work unsuccessfully as a consultant, and prefers a temporary position to none. One consultant who says he earns between $130,000 and $190,000 a year claims temp executive placement as one important source of his work.

Whether executive temp placement is consulting or not, it is certainly a resource that consultants should be aware of and one they may occasionally find expedient to take advantage of.

How They Work. Placement firms have enormous files of candidates which they enter into computer databases that can be sorted by experience, skill, or education. Firms can thus quite easily find several candidates close to the specifications of a client's request, and then screen them further.

For the candidate, the procedure is also simple, but quite undependable. Sending in your résumé gets you into the database, but you may never hear anything further. So you send in résumés to many firms, and therein lies to value of Snell's book on the subject.

Some temporary executive placement firms take on only temporary assignments. Most also are in related fields, such as executive search for permanent positions, and out-placement services, because these other services can have a synergistic benefit. Some put the candidate on the placement firm's payroll, which takes its 10 to 30 percent fee from your gross earnings. In other cases the executive is on the client's payroll or may be paid as a contractor.

Case Example. A leading and pioneering firm in this field is Interim Management Corp. (IMCOR) headquartered in Stamford, Connecticut with four branches in the United States. It has a database of 15,000 candidates, and a client database of 10,000. Placement requests are filled in ten days to six weeks. The firm receives a $2,500 retainer from a client for each search assignment. Of the 200 placements annually, 40 percent become permanent employees of the clients. IMCOR accepts only candidates who have been in the pay range of $75,000 or above.

Expert Referrals

Many consultants are asked from time to time to serve as experts in court proceedings and in other legal, insurance, business, and government matters. Expert referral agencies can be a source of these assignments. A flyer for one such agency, Expert Resources Inc., is shown on the next page. There is no charge to register with Expert Resources Inc.

Temporary Staffing Services

The prevalence of executive temporary placement firms is relatively new, but the use of temporary services for clerical and other less-than-executive positions has been a growing trend for several decades. Manpower, a leader in the field, reports annual revenues of $4 billion.

But there has been a tendency of late for temporary help services to take on more middle management and technical professionals, and even a few higher level executives. The National Association of Temporary and Staffing Services (NATSS) reports the following breakdown of percentages by position categories:

Percentage of Payroll by Industry Segment

40%	Office/Clerical
34%	Industrial
18%	Technical/Professional
6%	Health Care

The following are types of "Technical/Professional Positions":

Accountants
Attorneys
Computer Programmers
Doctors
Engineers
Middle and Senior Management
Paralegals
Sales and Marketing Professionals
... and more

HELP YOU NEED ... WHEN YOU NEED IT
SINCE 1979

- Regardless of your time constraints, a telephone call to one of our convenient local numbers, or to 800-383-4857, puts you in touch with the expert you need.

- ERI can call on experts in all fields for attorneys (plaintiff and defendant), insurance companies, government agencies, and corporations.

- ERI can assist in pinpointing the exact area of expertise you need.

- You will be promptly connected with an expert, or experts, so that you can make your decision regarding qualifications.

- Why spend valuable hours trying to locate the right expert in the right place without conflict of interest or time? Leave this to *EXPERTS ON EXPERTS* ®.

- These services are provided without charge unless you use our expert.

- Before deciding on an expert you will know what we know of the expert's background and rates (which include our administrative charge).

EXPERT RESOURCES INC.®
Experts on Experts ®
800-383-4857

Inside / Inside / Back / Front

Professional Specialty and Technical Occupations

Occupation	Number of Workers	Average Hourly Earnings
Commercial/Graphic Artists	1,712	17.63
Computer Systems Analysts	1,779	28.75
Designers	8,351	23.04
Engineers	10,243	28.54
Registered Nurses	6,164	21.98
Technical Writers	1,377	22.71
Computer Programmers	2,492	25.40
Drafters	2,492	13.64
Electrical and Electronic Technicians	6,853	10.32
Licensed Practical Nurses	4,908	14.30

More specific details about the hourly earnings and numbers of workers in "Professional Specialty and Technical Operations" are shown in the excerpt shown above from the *Occupational Compensation Survey: Temporary Help Supply Services— United States and Selected Metropolitan Areas, November 1944,* issued by the U.S. Department of Labor in May 1955.

Of course temp jobs are not consulting because the temp agencies are the real employers of the temp workers. But they do have in common the taking of assignments of limited duration. And temp assignments may offer the benefit of filling in time gaps between consulting engagements, especially for specialists like computer analysts and engineers, or for some retired persons who are performing consulting engagements on a part-time basis. The best way to find out about available temp jobs is to call agencies listed in the yellow pages. To learn more about the industry, contact its association, National Association of Temporary and Staffing Services, 119 South Saint Asaph Street, Alexandria, VA 22314.

Exec•U•Net

Exec•U•Net is an organization whose main purpose is to assist job seekers. It provides other services but its main benefit to members is biweekly lists of 250–300 job openings that it secures mostly from executive search firms. However, at least one consultant has found it a source of lucrative consulting work.

One of this firm's recent lists of openings included 22 entries in the consulting category, six of which were for jobs listing IMCOR, the executive temporary placement firm, as the source to contact. Most of the others were for permanent consulting positions in consulting firms.

Exec•U•Net limits its members to executives who have earned at least $75,000 annually. Membership costs $110 for three months, $170 for six months, and $290 for a full year. It was formed in 1988, and can be contacted at Exec•U•Net, 25 Van Zant Street, Suite 15–3, Norwalk, CT 06855.

Checklist

The following checklist is to help you review the issues in this chapter to evaluate whether you have considered the principles involved properly in your consulting plans or practice.

	Yes	No
Have you established a feeling of trust with your potential clients?		
Do you attend consulting association meetings?		
Do you attend technical association meetings?		
Are you an active participant in any association, e.g., hold officer or committee positions?		
Have you been asked to speak at association gatherings?		
Have you received referrals from association contacts?		
Have you given referrals to association contacts?		
Have you proposed writing articles on your special ideas or experiences?		
Do you have a system for following up contacts by phone?		
Do you have a system for following up contacts by mail?		
Do you keep notes on your contacts' hobbies, families, and other interests?		
Do you have a brochure that clearly explains your services and credentials?		
Have you prepared news releases about your activities of interest?		
Do your news releases conform to standard rules for acceptance by editors?		
Have you sent contacts and prospects articles of interest to them?		
Have you used newsletters as a marketing device?		
Do you keep a contact database coded by useful criteria?		
Have you asked to be included in published directories of consultants?		
Do you research the backgrounds of potential clients?		
Do you research the history and news about potential client organizations you plan to meet with?		
Do you question prospects as to their interests?		
Have you weighed whether and how to take appropriate advantage of consultant brokers and referral agencies?		

Associations and Networking Groups

Associations and networking are two separate, but closely related things. Various types of associations can benefit consultants for a variety of reasons. Being involved with associations is an effective means of networking, which is a primary part of marketing most consulting businesses. While networking is discussed throughout this book, this chapter reviews types of organizations that may be useful for networking purposes.

Participation in association activities can provide a wide variety of benefits for an independent consultant: learning approaches and techniques that can be helpful, making contacts that may lead to referrals, getting to know others who may help you with projects, enhancing your reputation as an expert, and so on. Associations are relatively inexpensive compared to the values they offer, but you can also spend too much nonbillable time with them and thereby reach a point of diminishing returns.

Association meetings can fulfill a real need for socializing for many solo independent consultants; some, being gregarious by nature, find that working solo has its lonely moments. Association gatherings can meet that need for social intercourse. In addition, meetings with peers who are also consultants or otherwise in your technical specialty can afford opportunities for discussing matters of mutual professional interest.

Two categories of associations are important to consultants: first, associations of consultants as such, and second, associations relating to the consultant's professional specialty, such as human resources, material handling, public speaking, or information systems. This chapter discusses leading organizations in these two categories, followed by ethics and certification features of associations. And finally, the chapter reviews additional thoughts on networking and networking groups.

Consulting Associations

The two leading management consulting associations are the Institute of Management Consultants, and the smaller and younger The National Bureau of Professional Consultants. Two significant consulting associations in specialized areas are the Independent Computer Consultants Association and the American Association of Healthcare Consultants.

A number of other consulting associations perform specialized functions, and they also are listed. Finally, three umbrella and trade organizations are discussed. These are not groups an independent consultant would join, but consultants should be aware of them as part of their understanding the consulting industry's structure.

Institute of Management Consultants (IMC)

The Institute of Management Consultants is the foremost and largest association for individual management consultants. Formed in 1968 to promote professionalism in consulting, it early established a certification process, and how has 2,600 members.

Membership Sources. Members include solo practitioners and consultants from small, medium, and large firms including many from the consulting branches of the "Big Six" public accounting firms. Individual practitioners form a large portion of the membership, and are particularly active in the meeting activities.

Benefits. A major benefit for the individual consultant, especially those new in the business, is the chance to meet with others in many specialties at meetings and the IMC's annual conferences. Most of the institute's 27 chapters hold monthly meetings. Topics at these gatherings usually relate to marketing and managing consulting businesses. And the individual acquaintances developed have resulted in many referrals and joint ventures to meet particular clients' needs.

Other benefits include special interest groups, a member directory, a newsletter, a *Journal of Management Consulting*, availability of health and errors and omissions insurance, opportunities for certification, and other services and products.

Referrals. Client inquiries are referred to qualified certified members, and the institute averages 500 such inquiries per year.

Dues and fees. Annual dues are $150, $300 for certified members. An application fee is $50. Certification fees are $250 for members, $600 for nonmembers.

Address. Institute of Management Consultants, 521 Fifth Avenue, 35th floor, New York, NY 10175, (212) 679–8262.

The National Bureau of Professional Management Consultants (NBPMC)

NBPMC was established in 1989 with the goal of creating a certification program and promoting MBA programs in management consulting. It has about 600 members. Those who do not meet NBPMC's certification standards for consulting experience and references may join the affiliated organization, American Association of Professional Consultants (AAPC).

Benefits. A bimonthly newsletter and the opportunity for certification.

Referrals. NBPMC received about 50 referrals from potential clients per year, and is planning a listing via an Internet database.

Dues and fees. Annual dues are $200.

Address. The National Bureau of Professional Management Consultants, 3577 Fourth Avenue, San Diego, CA 92103.

Independent Computer Consultants Association (ICCA)

The ICCA was established in 1976 to support independent computer consultants with services and benefits to assist them in their businesses.

Membership. Members must attest that a sizable part of their business comes from consulting services. Members may be individuals or firms. There are about 1,700 members.

Benefits. The association's services include a standard consulting contract form, health and liability and disability insurance programs, tax advice, a bimonthly newsletter, on-line services with networking opportunities, marketing aids, local chapter meetings, and an annual conference.

Referrals. Referrals are made by local chapters, which emphasize the value of exchanging information with one another.

Dues and fees. Dues range from $160 per year for an individual up to $275 for a firm with over ten people.

Address. Independent Computer Consultants Association, 11131 South Towne Square, Suite F, St. Louis, MO 63123.

American Association of Healthcare Consultants (AAHC)

Founded in 1949, AAHC has a membership of 250.

Membership. Individuals and firms that provide hospital and health care consulting assistance are eligible for membership, though there are rigid standards for membership acceptance.

Benefits. Benefit services include a conference, an annual membership directory, mailing lists, and a speaker's bureau.

Address. American Association of Healthcare Consultants, 11208 Waples Mill Road, Suite 109, Fairfax, VA 22030.

Other Specialized Consulting Groups

IMC and NBPMC are for management consultants, whereas ICCA and AAHC are specifically for computer and healthcare consultants, respectively.

Management consulting services (standard industrial classification 8742) is defined in part as "furnishing operating counsel and assistance to managements of private, nonprofit, and public organizations ... perform a variety of activities, such as strategic and organizational planning; financial planning and budgeting; marketing objectives and policies; information systems planning, evaluation, and selection; human resource policies and practices planning; and production scheduling and control planning." (*Standard Industrial Classification Manual—1987*, published by the Executive Office of the President, Office of Management and Budget.)

There are a great many associations of consultants in specialties that would not be considered management consulting as just defined. Independent consultants in fields with a viable association would do well to investigate the group's values and benefits and consider joining if it appears worthwhile. If you are not sure if an organization exists in your specialty, check the *Encyclopedia of Associations*, published annually by Gale Research Inc. in Detroit, Michigan, and available in most libraries. Here is a sampling of such associations:

American Consulting Engineers Council (ACEC)

American Association of Professional Bridal Consultants

American Society of Theater Consultants (ASTC)

Association of Image Consultants International (AICI)

Association of Professional Material Handling Consultants (APMHC)

Institute of Personal Image Consultants (IPIC)

National Association for Church Management Consultants (NACMC)

Society of Medical/Dental Management Consultants (SMD)

Society of Telecommunications Consultants (STC)

Each listing in the encyclopedia gives a brief summary of the association including its purpose, services offered, phone and address, and top executive's name.

Consulting Umbrella and Trade Associations

Although the three organizations described next are not groups an independent consultant would join, they are significant institutions in the consulting industry and, for that reason, you should be aware of them.

Council of Consulting Organizations (CCO). The CCO is an "umbrella" organization that coordinates the activities of The Association of Management Consulting Firms (ACME) and the Institute of Management Consultants, two leading organizations in the management consulting industry. These three organizations share the same headquarters in New York City.

The Association of Management Consulting Firms (ACME). ACME was founded in 1929 as the Association of Consulting Management Engineers. It has 42 members, including many of the larger management consulting firms and consulting branches of major public accounting firms. Established to enhance and monitor standards and practices in the field, it performs research, publishes a newsletter and other material, has a referral service, and does public relations.

International Council of Management Consulting Institutes (ICMCI). This council was formed in 1987 as a worldwide association of management consulting organizations, and has established a Uniform Body of Knowledge accepted among the institute's members. ICMCI's members are international management consulting institutes that certify professional consultants. The Institute of Management Consultants is the U.S. member.

Professional and Trade Associations

The associations just discussed are all related to consulting as such, and deal with the principles and practices of operating and marketing consulting businesses. Independent consultants derive many benefits from participating in these general consulting associations.

But most independent consultants should also be active in specialized groups that exchange ideas and experiences specific to their profession, whether it's engineering, human resources, marketing, or strategic planning. Every consultant, in addition to being a consultant, is an expert in one or more of these specialties.

One important reason to join a specialized group (discussed in more detail in the next chapter) is to stay on top technically in your field. Consultants must be up-to-date on the latest developments and technologies related to their consulting service.

Other reasons for participating in professional associations are similar to the reasons for belonging to consulting organizations: making acquaintances that may lead to referrals, finding out which companies are experiencing problems you might help them overcome, and socializing to lessen the feeling of loneliness some solo consultants experience.

Examples of specialized professional associations are listed next. If you are not familiar with the ones in your own specialties, thousands of these groups are listed in Gale Research Inc.'s *Encyclopedia of Associations*, available in most libraries.

American Association of Cereal Chemists (AACC)

American Society of Training and Development

Information Systems Security Association (ISSA)

Institute of Electrical and Electronics Engineers (IEEE)

National Speakers Association

Society of Human Resources Management

Code of Ethics

Practically every consulting and other professional association has a code of ethics, and makes some effort to see that its members comply with the code. These codes are one means for trying to assure clients and others that they will be dealt with fairly, honestly, and professionally.

The Code of Ethics of the Institute of Management Consultants is a model one, as it assures clients about the safeguarding of confidential information, impartial advice, qualified performance, pricing terms in advance, and realistic solutions. To enforce the code, IMC investigates complaints and metes out penalties when it determines that a member has not properly complied with the code. A copy of the IMC's Code of Ethics appears on page 108.

Certification

Certification by the Institute of Management Consultants is the most widely accepted consulting certification in the United States. IMC certifying practices are coordinated with those of the International Council of Management

CODE OF ETHICS

Clients

1. We will serve our clients with integrity, competence, and objectivity.

2. We will keep client information and records of client engagements confidential and will use proprietary client information only with the client's permission.

3. We will not take advantage of confidential client information for ourselves or our firms.

4. We will not allow conflicts of interest which provide a competitive advantage to one client through our use of confidential information from another client who is a direct competitor without that competitor's permission.

Engagements

5. We will accept only engagements for which we are qualified by our experience and competence.

6. We will assign staff to client engagements in accord with their experience, knowledge, and expertise.

7. We will immediately acknowledge any influences on our objectivity to our clients and will offer to withdraw from a consulting engagement when our objectivity or integrity may be impaired.

Fees

8. We will agree independently and in advance on the basis for our fees and expenses and will charge fees and expenses that are reasonable, legitimate, and commensurate with the services we deliver and the responsibility we accept.

9. We will disclose to our clients in advance any fees or commissions that we will receive for equipment, supplies or services we recommend to our clients.

Profession

10. We will respect the intellectual property rights of our clients, other consulting firms, and sole practitioners and will not use proprietary information or methodologies without permission.

11. We will not advertise our services in a deceptive manner and will not misrepresent the consulting profession, consulting firms, or sole practitioners.

12. We will report violations of this Code of Ethics.

The Council of Consulting Organizations, Inc. Board of Directors approved this Code of Ethics on January 8, 1991. The Institute of Management Consultants (IMC) is a division of the Council of Consulting Organizations, Inc.

IMC INSTITUTE OF MANAGEMENT CONSULTANTS
521 Fifth Avenue, 35th Floor, New York, NY 10175-3598

Consulting Institutes (ICMCI), which has about 20,000 Certified Management Consultants (CMCs) worldwide.

About 60 percent of IMC's 2,600 members have passed its Certified Management Consultant (CMC) requirements which include three years of full-time practice as a management consultant, client references, written summaries of client engagements, and a personal interview evaluating the candidate's competence as a consultant and in the specialized areas served.

Other organizations that have consulting certification are listed in the following table.

Association	Certification Awarded
Academy of Professional Consultants and Advisors (APCA)	CPC, Certified Professional Consultant
The Consultants Bureau	PMC, Professional Management Consultant
American Consultants League	CPC, Certified Professional Consultant
The National Bureau of Professional Management Consultants (NBPMC)	CPCM, Certified Professional Consultant to Management

Many nonconsulting professional associations also provide certification in their individual specialties. As an example, the Information Systems Security Association sponsors a certification process leading to the designation of Certified Information Systems Security Professional (CISSP).

In addition, some vendors of technical products, such as computer hardware and software, offer certification of competence in handling matters relating to their products, usually after the consultant completes an instructional program.

With all this, the proliferation of acronyms has become quite confusing. Unfortunately the abundance of certification acronyms people put after their names has somewhat lessened their effectiveness and confused many who are unfamiliar with them.

But for clients who are aware of an acronym's meaning, it demonstrates your interest in the field and assures clients of your competence in and dedication to your specialty.

Networking Groups

Networking has already been discussed as a primary means independent consultants use to secure clients and engagements.

Networking should always be a two-way street, and that can sometimes give the networking process a snowball effect. For example, if you introduce contacts to clients who become profitable for them, those business associates will often look for some opportunity to return that favor to you.

Participating in associations, as discussed earlier, is an excellent way to develop beneficial interpersonal relationships. But there are several other methods for developing contacts. Three are reviewed next: business groups, your own networking group, or a franchised network system.

Business Groups

Joining and participating in local business activities can benefit consultants whose potential clients are in the vicinity. Leading organizations with active local groups are Rotary, Kiwanis, and Chambers of Commerce.

Consultants who might find such groups especially effective include personal financial advisors, career counselors, or computer consultants who assist small businesses or individuals.

Forming Your Own Networking Group

Some individuals establish their own networking groups. Their purpose is to meet other business people and learn about their businesses, with the aim of turning such acquaintances into new business opportunities.
Such groups need an organizer to be the catalyst to get the group started and keep it on track. The groups usually have weekly or monthly get-togethers at a breakfast, lunch, or some other venue. Such groups may also help individual consultants learn about people who might provide a service to the consultant's business, such as an accountant, insurance broker, or attorney.

Joining a networking group may be worthwhile for an independent consultant. But it probably would not be time-effective to be the organizer of the group as doing that could take an undue amount of time away from other activities.

Franchise System

An organization called Business Network International headquartered in California was formed in 1985 to establish local networking franchises. These groups hold weekly meetings where members share their personal and business contacts. There are 430 chapters in the United States, Canada, and Puerto Rico.

Typical meetings are breakfast sessions at which members give a one-minute explanation of what they do and what sort of leads they are seeking. Most members are entrepreneurs, and the group is open to white-collar and blue-collar workers. Only one member in any business specialty is permitted in each chapter.

The owner of the company is Dr. Ivan Misner who is said to have a Ph.D. in networking and has published two books on the subject. Membership costs $215 annually, though shorter periods are possible. More information is available at (800) 825–8286.

Checklist The following checklist will help you review the issues in this chapter as they relate to your consulting plans or practice.

	Yes	No
Have you joined, or considered joining, a consulting association?		
Have you joined, or considered joining, a professional association in your specialty?		
Do you know which professional associations serve your consulting specialties?		
If you are a member of one or more associations, have you been an active participant?		
Have you achieved, or looked into, certification?		
Have you received client engagements from networking contacts?		
Have you been a source of business for one or more of your networking contacts?		
Have you developed a beneficial joint venture with an association acquaintance?		

How to Stay on Top Technically and Professionally

Consultants must be competent and knowledgeable about current developments in their fields of specialization. The ideal for a consultant is to be perceived as a guru, a leading counselor in the business or technical area.

Certain people have in the past achieved eminent reputations by being the best, most pioneering experts in their individual specialties. Such gurus include:

Reengineering	James A. Champy
Quality management	D. Edwards Deming
Management strategies	Peter Drucker
Investment know-how	Louis Rukeyser
Positive thinking	Norman Vincent Peale
Industrial engineering	Frank and Lillian Gilbreth

This chapter is adapted from the article "How to Stay Competitive Professionally" by Douglas B. Hoyt in *Systems Development Management*. (New York: Auerbach Publications), © 1995 Warren, Gorham & Lamont. Used with permission.

Few consultants attain such worldwide eminence. But all consultants must be discerned as fully competent and knowledgeable in the latest developments within their specialties, whatever they may be. Each of the six successful consultants profiled in Appendix A has developed a reputation as a leader in some niche, such as cereal food engineering, membership club computer systems, or international business consulting.

Some consultants begin by establishing a strong local reputation. Barbara Niles just started as a consultant in advisory services for Apple computers. When my eight-year-old Macintosh would not print, she came over and fixed it promptly, and I happily paid for her services. Barbara also provided helpful suggestions and service to my neighbor. Both my neighbor and I tell anyone who asks about help with an Apple or Macintosh, "Call in Barbara Niles. She's the best around." Barbara Niles has achieved the guru image in her specialty in our Hartsdale, New York, vicinity. The knowledge she needed to establish her reputation she achieved by working for an Apple distributor, attending many Apple conventions, and reading all the literature she could, leading a local Apple user's group, and networking with others in the field.

This chapter will review methods for consultants to stay on top technically and professionally, as well as maintaining the reputation of being on top. It will cover budgeting your time, areas to watch, networking, associations, trade shows, magazines and newspapers, books and libraries, technical publication services, Internet and bulletin boards, professional seminar providers, demonstrating and reinforcing leadership, and balancing your personal and professional life.

Budgeting Your Time

New developments constantly occur in the many areas of consulting specialization, from health management to human resources. Change happens in the computer field at a record-high pace. Therefore, if you do not constantly keep current, you lose your reputation as a leading expert in your specialty, and you lose your competitive advantage over other consultants. The consultants who show they are best equipped to apply the latest proven approaches are the ones most likely to be selected for engagements.

But staying on top professionally takes a lot of time and effort, which may even impinge on your personal life and on time available for billable work. In a certain sense, time spent learning and keeping current is a part of your marketing effort because doing so is necessary to maintain your reputation as a leader in your specialty. Therefore, you must weigh carefully the many possible ways to stay ahead, and how much effort you should apply to each at any particular time. To best meet your objectives, select those learning methods that will help you reach your goals most effectively, and then work vigorously at the chosen approaches.

Areas to Watch

The areas in which to keep current include your specialty or specialties, the particular industry or industries you serve, and business generally. Business trends are hard to predict. But you can anticipate them by looking at new approaches that have evolved in the last decade or two.

Consultant's Technical Specialty

Recent shifts have included:

In computers, from mainframes, minicomputers, and personal computers (PCs) to client/servers, and Internet.

In production control, to just-in-time parts deliveries.

In quality management, to 100% acceptance.

Industry Served by Consultant

In many industries, innovative applications have helped some companies to achieve a competitive edge. These include:

Electronic data interchange (EDI) in manufacturing industries

Asynchronous transfer modes (ATMs) in the banking industry

Computerized tracking systems in the trucking and package delivery business

Automated reservations systems in the airline industry

Business—New Directions

Recent business and managerial trends include:

Reengineering

Downsizing

Restructuring

Mergers and acquisitions

Divestments and separations by types of business

Quality improvement and control

The above technical, industry, and business developments exemplify types of trends a consultant must be aware of. The many possible ways to stay on top of technical and business developments will be reviewed next.

Networking

Networking is the cultivation of friends and acquaintances who may be of help in the future. Networking assumes reciprocity, or mutually beneficial relationships. It means engaging in conversations with people who have knowledge and ideas in the areas you have targeted for your professional advancement.

Contacts can be friends, peers, subordinates, superiors, vendors, teachers, social acquaintances, bulletin board contacts, and people you meet at association meetings, conferences, or trade shows. You can gain information from these people by asking them about their experiences and ideas in their areas of expertise. Pay close attention to their answers and continue the conversation with well-thought-out questions that display your intellectual curiosity. People generally are flattered to be asked to explain things they know about to an interested inquirer, so they usually respond willingly. They, in turn, gain from the opportunity to ask questions of their own about matters that interest them.

For consultants, networking is a principal means for securing contacts that lead to new engagements and new clients. Listening also is key to developing client interest, effectiveness in negotiation, interview success, and showing interest in your business acquaintances and contacts.

But both networking and listening can be valuable methods for keeping abreast of current developments in business and technical matters. Although consultants try and hope to be viewed as highly knowledgeable about their business and technical specialties, most everyone consultants meet with has some knowledge or understanding that could broaden the consultants' store of information.

So it is wise to use networking as a two-way street—learning from others as well as letting them know about you.

Associations

A primary purpose of most professional associations is to help members gain knowledge and ideas in their particular areas of expertise, especially with respect to recent and current developments. This is done through monthly meetings, regional one- or two-day conferences, annual national or international conferences of three days or more, technical journals, research, traveling seminars, and other activities.

Association meetings can be an important means for learning about technical matters and developments from those who have special knowledge about them. As gatherings of people with similar concerns, they are an excellent source for making networking contacts and discussing matters of mutual interest. Associations are also, of course, good places for developing and practicing leadership and speaking skills by accepting committee work, committee leadership and officer positions, and requests to lead meetings.

Computer User Groups

User groups in the computer field, which represents a major portion of consultants, are like associations in many respects and have similar benefits. However, user groups are limited to people who use a specific vendor's products. These groups are organizationally and financially separate from the vendors, and vendors attend their gatherings only when invited. However, the vendors support the groups and may assist them when asked.

User groups offer the same benefits as associations: opportunities to network, learn about technical developments and anticipated product releases, share experiences in problem solving, and practice leadership in the group's management and administration.

Trade Shows

Trade shows of computer or other industry product areas are usually annual events of several days' duration in convention center locations. In addition to offering seminars in the latest technology trends, these shows bring together representatives of vendors of the industry's products and services. Competing vendors set up displays and booths where their sales people vigorously promote their products' and services' beneficial features.

Trade shows are great places to develop a sense of what is new in the field, to get information about particular product features and plans, and to make contacts that may be useful in later investigations and research.

Vendors

Vendors are an outstanding source for getting to know what is new, what is on the horizon, and the pros and cons of different products. This applies to computer consultants, engineers in production management, and many others who apply technologies or products that are evolving technically.

Vendors' success depends on developing effective methodologies, so they are motivated to explain their products—and competitors' products—to highlight strengths, weaknesses, and features that set them apart. Even though vendors cannot ethically reveal proprietary information about their competitors, they often indicate directions of competing companies in their industry.

Business lunches and vendor-sponsored seminars and announcements are also potential sources of information on how products really work—information left "between the lines" in promotional material.

Magazines and Newspapers

Magazines are available in abundance, many covering quite thoroughly very narrow areas of technical specialization. They are an essential resource for keeping current about present and future technology and products. These magazines discuss in depth new techniques and products, and what users are saying about them; publications also contain editorial comments and opinions. Many explain customers' applications, how they work, their benefits, and problems encountered.

Magazines are also a source for learning about upcoming conferences, conventions, and trade shows. Many magazines are free to subscribers who are professionals in the magazine's area of specialization, because sufficient income is provided by the magazine's advertisers. The following is a list of some computer magazines that you may subscribe to without charge.

Free Computer-Related Magazines

Application Development Trends
Ideas on, and examples of, computer applications system innovations
Monthly

Beyond Computing
"Integrating Business & Information Technology"
Nine times per year

CIO, The Magazine for Information Executives
Issues of interest to senior systems executives
Twenty-one times per year

Client/Server Computing
"For Managers of Next Generation Information Systems"
Monthly

Communications Week
"The Newspaper for Enterprise Networking"
Weekly

Computer Design
Technical aspects of hardware design and digital equipment and systems
Monthly

Computerworld
"The Newspaper of Information Systems Management"
Weekly
Subscription includes bimonthly *Client/Server Journal*

Datamation
"Strategic solutions for enterprise computing professionals"
Monthly

DEC Professional
Products and trends in the Digital Equipment Corp. market
Monthly

Document Management
"The Magazine on Automation of Documentation Management"
Bimonthly

Enterprise Internetworking Journal
Internetwoking issues for IBM mainframes
Monthly

Enterprise Reengineering
"The National Publication for BPR"
Monthly

Enterprise Systems Journal
Technical and how-to articles on IBM and large mainframe systems
Monthly

HP Professional
Technology and systems related to Hewlett-Packard products
Monthly

ID Systems
"The Magazine of Automated Data Collection"
Monthly

Industrial Computing Plus Programmable Controls
Computer issues relating to manufacturing applications
Monthly

Information Week
"For Business and Technology Managers"

InfoWorld
Personal computer systems
Weekly

Internetwork
Multivendor networks, open systems, industry standards
Monthly

IW—Imaging World
"Image, Document Management & Workflow News"
Monthly

Macworld
"The Macintosh® Authority"
Monthly

Managing Office Technology
"Integrated Technology & Human Resources for Total Office Quality"
Monthly

Midrange Systems
IBM AS/400 and RS/6000 news and technology
Biweekly

New Media Magazine
News about innovative products and systems
Monthly

News & Review
News about PICK/UNIX/DBMS related systems
Monthly

Office Systems
"The Voice of the Small to Midsize Company"
Monthly

Personal Engineering & Instrumentation News
Technical and scientific PC systems
Monthly

Publish
"The Magazine for Electronic Publishing
     Professionals"
Monthly

Relational Database
"Focusing on Enterprise-Wide Database
     Management & Computing"
Bimonthly

RS/Magazine
For users of IBM's RISC/6000 systems
Monthly

Scientific Computing & Automation
"Technology for the Scientific and Engineering
     Workplace"
Monthly

Software Development
Emphasizes how to manage the software devel-
     opment process
Monthly

Software Magazine
"For Managers of Corporate Software"
Monthly

Upside
"The Business Magazine for the Technology
     Elite"
Monthly

For general business reading, newspapers such as *The Wall Street Journal* and *The New York Times* have good coverage abut managerial trends and technical developments, as well as some activities of interest in individual industries. Magazines such as *Business Week, Fortune*, and *Forbes* also cover these matters, often in more detail. Other magazines cover business and technical developments in individual industries.

Most professional associations publish periodical journals intended to cover current technology issues and new directions in their associations' individual specialties. These journals usually also review case examples of applications, their problems, and how to surmount obstacles. Most of these journals are included with the cost of membership in the association, but nonmembers can subscribe.

Books and Libraries

Books evolve too slowly to be on the cutting edge of technology. But they are an excellent source for gathering background on a particular topic because books cover subjects more completely than periodicals. This is especially true of handbooks, which by definition encompass a wide range of topics and are structured for ready reference—with many headings, indexes, and detailed tables of contents.

Bookstores and libraries are two traditional sources of information. Libraries are becoming increasingly easy and efficient to use. Computerized systems readily locate items by title, author, or key words. Small libraries have databases of what neighboring libraries have; if you find material through the database, the smaller library can request that material from the appropriate libraries. Larger libraries may have a variety of CD-ROMs with indexes to government data or other specialized fields of knowledge. Most library computerized reference systems print out selected reference data, and many print out abstracts of articles in periodicals.

The one drawback to all these reference systems is that they differ from library to library and from CD- ROM to CD-ROM, so the consultant who seldom uses them may need to invest a lot of time to become familiar with each new indexing system.

One advantage is that library staff members are usually dedicated and willing to help. Their availability is also enhanced by the computerized reference systems that have lessened the demands on staff time.

Technical Publication Services

Technical publication services, such as Auerbach Publications in the computer management area, cover fields by function with a practical, hands-on approach. Auerbach's lines include handbooks, which give comprehensive coverage of major areas of information management, loose-leaf services, and newsletters.

A main product is the Auerbach Information Management Series, which contains eight loose-leaf binder services, supplemented bimonthly to keep the subject coverage up-to-date. The binders, which are also available on disk and CD-ROM, combine the benefits of books and periodicals; they cover the full range of a broad subject area, and reflect current facts and ideas more promptly than a book can. The electronic formats enable rapid searches by key words, and can be downloaded readily for further analysis or presentations.

Internet and Bulletin Boards

Bulletin boards offer the latest methods for networking and for finding people eager to exchange experience and ideas on subjects of common interest. Consultants can secure answers to problems that may not be readily found in literature or even among business associates and acquaintances because a multitude of bulletin board users share information via electronic means. Gathering information electronically is efficient because the bulletin board allows for networking without the bother of actually meeting the participants in person and making the small talk such relationships usually entail.

Similarly Internet can be an effective means for securing information. The user, however, must first master the methodology for using the system, and be aware of all the types of information available and where to get them.

The problem with these electronic sources is that bulletin boards and the Internet can become time-consuming diversions, and can lead to excessive search time.

Other commercial electronic data sources, such as America Online and CompuServe, also access business and technical information. Advantages include convenience and speed in securing articles and data from magazines, newspapers, encyclopedias, and other sources.

Professional Seminar Providers

Many organizations conduct computer seminars in various cities; these usually last one to three days. Some of these organizations are listed in the table below.

Organizations that Produce Seminars

Alexander Hamilton Institute
605 Grand Avenue
PO Box 794
Hacketstown, NJ 07840

American Management Association
PO Box 169
Saranac Lake, NY 12983

Center for Advanced Professional Development
1820 East Gary Street, Suite 110
Santa Ana, CA 92705

Data-Tech Institute
PO Box 2429
Clifton, NJ 07015

INTERPRISE Networking Services
Data Network Training
1999 Broadway, Suite 700
Denver, CO 80202

MIS Training Institute
498 Concord Street
Framingham, MA 01701–2357

SkillPath Seminars
P.O. Box 2768
Mission, KS 66201–2768

Demonstrating and Reinforcing Leadership

Leadership can be practiced by volunteering for and accepting leadership work in associations and user groups, and by taking advantage of their certification processes. Another highly effective way to improve and display both technical knowledge and leadership skills is by developing speeches to give at meetings and by writing articles for publication. Finally, taking the initiative in researching and developing innovative applications is the best way of all to offer proof of technical and business expertise.

Association and User Group Leadership

Most associations and user group chapters are eager to find members who are willing to work on various projects—newsletters, programs, membership, and conference planning, for example. Reliable members are often asked to be committee leaders and officers at regional, national, and international levels.

Though these activities and positions offer no salaries, costs of materials are normally reimbursed. The benefits for the consultant include networking and learning; the most important value emphasized here, however, is the practice at performing leadership roles.

As people move up in these organizations, they must delegate responsibilities to others. This means they must use persuasion and encouragement to motivate others to volunteer because monetary rewards are not available as incentives. In consulting work, persuasion and encouragement are the most effective means for securing and carrying out engagements.

Computer-Related Certifications

Chapter 6 discussed certifications related to consulting capabilities, other technical association certifications, and certifications from vendors. There are several computer-related certifications, three of which are reviewed here.

The Institute for Certification of Computing Professionals (ICCP) maintains a certification program to encourage and verify appropriate knowledge and competence in computer areas. The ICCP goals of continuing professional development are

1. to maintain professional competence,

2. to update existing knowledge and skills, and

3. to attain new or additional knowledge and skills.

To become a Certified Computing Professional (CCP) under ICCP, a practitioner must verify a minimum level of experience and pass a series of tests to validate competency in the field. Preparatory review courses and educational materials are available on audiocassettes, computer disks, and in workbook formats.

To remain certified, the CCP must demonstrate continued learning and professional activity by documenting attendance at seminars, conferences, university courses; by speaking and writing on computer topics; and in other ways. An alternative to supplying documentation is to retake the entrance tests after a three-year period. There are 50,000 CCPs today.

The ICCP has evolved from the combined efforts of associations that started to establish separate certifications some years ago. It is run by the 12 associations below, each of which designates two ICCP board members. They are:

Association for Computing Machinery (ACM)—(212) 626-0500

Association for Systems Management—(216) 243-6900

Association for Women in Computing—(415) 905-4663

Black Data Processing Associates (National)— (800) 727–BDPA

Canadian Information Processing Society—(416) 593-4040

Coleman Computer Association—(619) 465-4063

COMMON: A Users Group—(312) 644-6610

Data Processing Management Association—(708) 825-8124

Independent Computer Consultants Association— (314) 997-4633

International Society for Technology in Education— (503) 346-4414

MicroComputer Managers Association—(212) 787-1122

Network Professional Association—(801) 429-7227

Further information can be obtained from the Institute for Certification of Computing Professionals, 2200 East Devon Avenue, Suite 268, Des Plaines, IL 60018-4503.

The Information Systems Security Association (ISSA) joined with other organizations to establish a Certified Information Systems Security Professional (CISSP) designation. For further information about that certification program and its seminars, contact CISSP's overseeing organization, the International Systems Security Certification Consortium, Inc., also known as (ISC)^2, at (508) 393-2296.

The Information Systems Audit and Control Association administers a Certified Information Systems Audit (CISA) program. Acceptance is based on meeting experience requirements and passing an examination. Preparation and review material is available from the association, phone (708) 253–1545.

Speaking and Writing

Speaking and writing assignments are easier to come by than many people think, and they can have many benefits professionally. Members of associations or user groups can readily create opportunities to speak by offering to give a talk about an experience or skill of interest to other members. After delivering the talk, the speaker can write about the session and send the piece to publications, which are often glad to receive material of interest to their subscribers. These publications usually pay modest honorariums for articles upon publication.

Benefits from speaking and writing include supporting your image as an authority in the field, which can lead to more offers to speak and write. Most importantly, public speaking enhances your ability to explain things clearly and to persuade an audience—talents that are of great value to a consultant. These skills are needed for making consulting proposal presentations and for verbally summarizing an engagement's results to clients.

A further benefit is a snowballing effect with the networking process. People who have spoken at meetings and published are sought out by others who are looking for knowledgeable people with whom they can exchange experiences and views. Though the process of giving talks often starts with local association or user groups, those occasions can lead to presentations to larger groups at conferences, seminars, trade shows, and other gatherings.

Another beneficial by-product is the feedback from audiences at such sessions. Often, during question and answer periods, audience members explain their related experiences, challenge the speaker's premises, or bring to light important new aspects of the issues being discussed, all of which can broaden the speaker's knowledge.

Pioneering Research and Development Applications

When a promising new technology or approach appears on the horizon, you can sometimes make that innovation an opportunity to become a successful pioneer. For example, you might convince a client or potential client to support your research and assist you in making the new approach workable for the client's organization. If and when the new application becomes successful, the client would gain a competitive edge by being an early innovator with an improved process. And you could add this pioneering joint achievement to your credentials, supporting your reputation as a leader in your field.

In addition, the successful joint effort would foster a bond with the client who may offer you further engagements in the future. And other clients might then ask you to spearhead the application of the new successful methodology at their organizations.

Balancing Personal and Professional Life

Pursuing fully all the options outlined in this chapter in addition to running a consulting business would require 48 or more hours a day—an impossibility, of course. Therefore, how much time you devote to these self-training efforts depends on the needs of your family, your personal life, the time demands of your business, including marketing, and the intensity of your desire to get ahead. Remember that some of the learning methods are part of the marketing process, such as networking; others are not, such as reading periodicals.

Many professional and educational activities cannot be done during normal working hours. Association dinner meetings, committee meetings, writing articles, and weekend travel to and from trade shows are some of the things that must be done outside of the normal work week. They all lessen the time available for family matters and personal activities.

Because of these time considerations, you must consider carefully the activities best suited to meet your career and business goals.

Checklist

The following checklist will help you review the issues covered in this chapter as they relate to your consulting plans or practice.

	Yes	No
Are you up-to-date with the latest developments in your specialty?		
Do you regularly read or scan major periodicals in your field?		
Have you offered to make presentations at association gatherings?		
Have you written articles for publication in periodicals?		
Do you attend trade shows and ask many questions about products and services?		
Do you seek leadership positions in associations?		
Have you attended seminars to increase your knowledge of your specialty?		
Have you used vendors as a source of knowledge about current developments?		
Have you taken proper advantage of free periodicals in your specialty?		
Are you familiar with resources available on Internet, bulletin boards, and databases?		
Have you sought to pioneer new methods or approaches with your clients?		
Have you analyzed the effectiveness of your learning approaches?		
Is your learning plan well balanced with your family and personal needs?		

How to Manage Your Back Office and Business Affairs

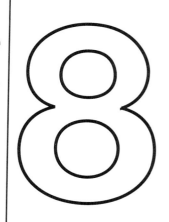

This chapter will cover how to keep your business operating, how to manage your financial affairs, including the all-important provision for what are called "fringe benefits" in employment situations. While securing clients and doing professional work on their behalf is the main thrust of any consulting business, proper records must be maintained for management control purposes, taxes must be paid and kept to legal minimums, and suitable provisions must be made to cover medical needs and retirement plans. Many independent consultants take care of these matters themselves, but others find it worthwhile to use advisors for help with accounting, taxes, legal questions, and computers. These issues are reviewed in this chapter.

Accounting, Tax, Legal, and Computer Advisors

You may be able to begin and manage your own independent consulting business without retaining any accounting, tax, legal, or computer advisors. If your practice is simple, small, and you have confidence in taking care of these matters yourself, handling them alone can save money and also give you the feeling of personal and direct control over these affairs.

But there are many benefits to seeking sound advice and assistance in these matters. Doing so can keep you from making serious mistakes, may save you time, and may give you the peace of mind that an expert's counsel can provide. Indeed, as a consultant, you are in the business of selling advice and problem solving to others. If you form a partnership or corporation, legal assistance is probably essential.

Some things to consider in deciding whether and when to retain each of these advisors are outlined below.

Accounting

Accounting advice and assistance can range from the bare minimum to doing the whole thing. The minimum is to have the accountant prepare your year-end tax returns from your records, or review the tax returns you prepare for accuracy and appropriateness. Some consultants have their accountants prepare monthly financial statements as well as their year-end statements and annual tax returns.

Accountants also can assist in setting up the accounting system for a new consulting business. This service assures the accountant of proper controls, and enables the client to capitalize on the accountant's experience and thereby avoid the trial and error of designing an accounting system unaided.

If the accountant has computer systems experience and the consultant is not strong in computer know-how, using that accountant's computer advice, along with the accountant's other services, can be helpful.

For a proprietorship, the main requirement is to keep track of expenses so they can be reported on IRS Schedule C, Profit or Loss From Business, a copy of which is shown on page 129-130. This means summarizing your costs in the IRS categories, e.g., advertising, office expenses, and supplies. These records may be maintained by hand on a columnar worksheet, on Quicken, or other accounting program, or on a spreadsheet (see a Consultant's Financial Spreadsheet on page 131).

When a consultant's business is more complex than the simple proprietorship, accounting assistance may be necessary, though the degree of support would depend on the circumstances. Partnerships and corporations have different tax reporting requirements. And if the consulting business has employees, an accountant would most certainly be helpful in preparing the necessary federal, state, and local payroll reports and payments.

SCHEDULE C (Form 1040) Department of the Treasury Internal Revenue Service (O)	**Profit or Loss From Business** (Sole Proprietorship) ▶ Partnerships, joint ventures, etc., must file Form 1065. ▶ **Attach to Form 1040 or Form 1041.** ▶ **See Instructions for Schedule C (Form 1040).**	OMB No. 1545-0074 **1995** Attachment Sequence No. **09**

Name of proprietor | Social security number (SSN)

A Principal business or profession, including product or service (see page C-1) | **B** Enter principal business code
(see page C-6) ▶ | | | |

C Business name. If no separate business name, leave blank. | **D** Employer ID number (EIN), if any | | | | | | |

E Business address (including suite or room no.) ▶ ....
  City, town or post office, state, and ZIP code

F Accounting method: **(1)** ☐ Cash   **(2)** ☐ Accrual   **(3)** ☐ Other (specify) ▶ ....

G Method(s) used to value closing inventory: **(1)** ☐ Cost   **(2)** ☐ Lower of cost or market   **(3)** ☐ Other (attach explanation)   **(4)** ☐ Does not apply (if checked, skip line H)

		Yes	No
H	Was there any change in determining quantities, costs, or valuations between opening and closing inventory? If "Yes," attach explanation		
I	Did you "materially participate" in the operation of this business during 1995? If "No," see page C-2 for limit on losses. . .		

J If you started or acquired this business during 1995, check here . . . . ▶ ☐

Part I   Income

1	Gross receipts or sales. **Caution:** *If this income was reported to you on Form W-2 and the "Statutory employee" box on that form was checked, see page C-2 and check here* . . . . ▶ ☐	**1**	
2	Returns and allowances	**2**	
3	Subtract line 2 from line 1	**3**	
4	Cost of goods sold (from line 40 on page 2)	**4**	
5	**Gross profit.** Subtract line 4 from line 3	**5**	
6	Other income, including Federal and state gasoline or fuel tax credit or refund (see page C-2) . .	**6**	
7	**Gross income.** Add lines 5 and 6 . . . . ▶	**7**	

Part II   Expenses. Enter expenses for business use of your home **only** on line 30.

8	Advertising	**8**		**19**	Pension and profit-sharing plans	**19**	
9	Bad debts from sales or services (see page C-3) . .	**9**		**20**	Rent or lease (see page C-4):		
10	Car and truck expenses (see page C-3) . .	**10**			**a** Vehicles, machinery, and equipment .	**20a**	
11	Commissions and fees. . .	**11**			**b** Other business property . .	**20b**	
12	Depletion.	**12**		**21**	Repairs and maintenance . .	**21**	
13	Depreciation and section 179 expense deduction (not included in Part III) (see page C-3) . .	**13**		**22**	Supplies (not included in Part III) .	**22**	
				23	Taxes and licenses	**23**	
14	Employee benefit programs (other than on line 19) . . .	**14**		**24**	Travel, meals, and entertainment:		
15	Insurance (other than health) .	**15**			**a** Travel	**24a**	
16	Interest:				**b** Meals and entertainment		
	a Mortgage (paid to banks, etc.) .	**16a**			**c** Enter 50% of line 24b subject to limitations (see page C-4) .		
	b Other	**16b**			**d** Subtract line 24c from line 24b .	**24d**	
17	Legal and professional services	**17**		**25**	Utilities	**25**	
				26	Wages (less employment credits) .	**26**	
18	Office expense	**18**		**27**	Other expenses (from line 46 on page 2)	**27**	

28	**Total expenses** before expenses for business use of home. Add lines 8 through 27 in columns. ▶	**28**	
29	Tentative profit (loss). Subtract line 28 from line 7	**29**	
30	Expenses for business use of your home. Attach **Form 8829**	**30**	
31	**Net profit or (loss).** Subtract line 30 from line 29.		
	• If a profit, enter on **Form 1040, line 12,** and ALSO on **Schedule SE, line 2** (statutory employees, see page C-5). Estates and trusts, enter on Form 1041, line 3. • If a loss, you MUST go on to line 32.	**31**	
32	If you have a loss, check the box that describes your investment in this activity (see page C-5). • If you checked 32a, enter the loss on **Form 1040, line 12,** and ALSO on **Schedule SE, line 2** (statutory employees, see page C-5). Estates and trusts, enter on Form 1041, line 3. • If you checked 32b, you MUST attach **Form 6198.**	**32a** ☐ All investment is at risk. **32b** ☐ Some investment is not at risk.	

For Paperwork Reduction Act Notice, see Form 1040 instructions.   Cat. No. 11334P   **Schedule C (Form 1040) 1995**

Schedule C (Form 1040) 1995   Page **2**

Part III   **Cost of Goods Sold** (see page C-5)

33	Inventory at beginning of year. If different from last year's closing inventory, attach explanation	33	
34	Purchases less cost of items withdrawn for personal use	34	
35	Cost of labor. Do not include salary paid to yourself	35	
36	Materials and supplies	36	
37	Other costs	37	
38	Add lines 33 through 37	38	
39	Inventory at end of year	39	
40	**Cost of goods sold.** Subtract line 39 from line 38. Enter the result here and on page 1, line 4	40	

Part IV   **Information on Your Vehicle.** Complete this part **ONLY** if you are claiming car or truck expenses on line 10 and are not required to file Form 4562 for this business. See the instructions for line 13 on page C-3 to find out if you must file.

41   When did you place your vehicle in service for business purposes? (month, day, year) ▶ ..../......../........ .

42   Of the total number of miles you drove your vehicle during 1995, enter the number of miles you used your vehicle for:

a   Business ....   b Commuting ....   c Other ....

43   Do you (or your spouse) have another vehicle available for personal use? . . . .   ☐ Yes   ☐ No

44   Was your vehicle available for use during off-duty hours? . . . .   ☐ Yes   ☐ No

45a   Do you have evidence to support your deduction? . . . .   ☐ Yes   ☐ No
 b   If "Yes," is the evidence written? . . . .   ☐ Yes   ☐ No

Part V   **Other Expenses.** List below business expenses not included on lines 8–26 or line 30.

....	
....	
....	
....	
....	
....	
....	
....	
....	
46 Total other expenses. Enter here and on page 1, line 27	46	

♻ *Printed on recycled paper*   *U.S.GPO:1995-389-198

Consultant's Financial Spreadsheet

Codes: 17 = Professional Services
18 = Office Expenses

Date	Description	Check No.	22 Supplies	18 Phone	24a Travel	24b Meals & Entnmt	27 Dues & Publ.	27 Seminar	Code	Other	TOTAL EXPENSES	INCOME	PROFIT

1995

Exercise: Accounting Worksheet or Spreadsheet

Prepare a layout for a proprietorship consulting business accounting record. Use an accounting columnar worksheet, or a computer spreadsheet.

Select the column headings by identifying expense categories on Part II of IRS Schedule C (Form 1040) which you will need for your business. Be guided by the "Consultants' Financial Spreadsheet" and the "IRS Schedule C, Profit or Loss From Business."

Tax Advisor

Your tax advisor, if you have one, is most likely to be your accountant. Accountants can provide adequate counsel on tax matters for most independent consultants. In setting up your business, however, if you are considering the options of partnership or S or C corporation, your attorney may be the one advising you on the tax consequences of choosing a certain legal structure for your business.

You will probably depend on your accountant or attorney for any special tax advice, unless you should happen to run into some complex tax issue that requires a tax specialist, who could either be an attorney or a CPA.

Legal Advisor

Legal advice is expensive, so it is best avoided if not needed. But there are at least three situations in which legal counsel is necessary. They are (1) if you want to set up a partnership or C corporate structure, (2) if you have client engagements which are long-term or involve questions of rights (such as copyright rights in computer programs or in implementation and maintenance of computer systems), or (3) if you get into trouble, such as when someone threatens to sue you.

Even if you do not anticipate any of these three situations that require legal services, it is wise to be aware of an attorney or attorneys whom you might trust and feel comfortable with if the need arises. If someone does threaten to sue, you don't want to be saying to yourself, "I wish I knew a good lawyer."

How do you find an attorney (or an accountant or tax expert)? By networking. Ask acquaintances or friends you trust what lawyers (or accountants or tax experts) they have found to be reliable and competent.

Computer Advisor

Over half the consultants are in computer specialties, according to Department of Commerce statistics cited in chapter 1. Therefore, most independent consultants are skilled in planning and operating computer systems, which are becoming more and more important to the success of small businesses, including consulting businesses.

Most independent consultants find that a computer is necessary or worthwhile for accounting, correspondence, proposals, newsletters, databases of clients and prospects, financial planning and analysis, preparing flyers and promotional material, searching for data on the Internet, e-mail, and all sorts of other uses.

So, if you are not experienced or comfortable with computer systems and plan to use a computer, it is wise to have an advisor to help you use your computer to the best advantage for your business. This advisor can help you make decisions about what hardware and software to buy, help you install and operate them, and then be a troubleshooter when problems arise.

Some inexperienced computer users can get by with "free" advice from vendors, friends and acquaintances, and user groups. But computer systems are of sufficient importance to a consulting business that it is often advisable to have the support of a professional computer consultant.

Computer Resources

Starting from scratch and setting up computer operations for a consulting business can be a daunting task. You may have the basics already in place. If not, it may be best to proceed one phase at a time. You might start with word processing and accounting, then add a modem, database, spreadsheet, and finally desktop publishing.

Choosing software and hardware can be confusing because there are so many options, each with varied pros and cons. So advice from your accountant or a trusted computer consultant can save you the time you would spend on research, talking to vendors, and trial and error.

Accounting

Accounting can be done on a spreadsheet, as in the case shown in the Consultant's Financial Spreadsheet on page 000. Quicken accounting software serves many small businesses well in making budgets and financial statements, paying bills, and performing other accounting operations. Other systems like Peachtree also are popular and provide for double-entry accounting, which Quicken does not.

Modem

A modem is necessary for sending and receiving e-mail and for using Internet and commercial databases such as America Online.

Spreadsheet   IBM's Lotus and Microsoft's Excel are the two most popular spreadsheet programs. Spreadsheets can be useful for financial analyses, and comparing alternative "what if?" situations, as described in chapter 2 under "Making a Plan." A spreadsheet used as a basic accounting record for a proprietorship is shown on page 000, Consultant's Financial Spreadsheet.

Database   A database is helpful, if not necessary, for keeping a mailing list for newsletters or promotional material, as well as for storing information about past clients, potential clients, and referral contacts. Databases can be coded by categories—e.g., potential clients or newsletter addressees—and they can be sorted in many ways, such as alphabetically by name, numerically by zip code, or by category codes.

Word Processing   Word processing is the tool for writing letters, proposals, reports, and other documents. The most popular program, and almost an industry standard, is Microsoft's Word, although WordPerfect is running second and is still much used.

Desktop Publishing   Word processing programs can produce an acceptable newsletter. But if your newsletter is an important product or merchandising tool, consider buying a good desktop publishing program that will allow you to produce a more professional looking product. QuarkXPress and Adobe's Pagemaker are two popular desktop publishing programs.

Also, if you plan to be in the speaking business, Microsoft's PowerPoint software can help you prepare effective presentation materials with graphic features. PowerPoint can be purchased in a package called Microsoft Office, which includes Microsoft's Word wordprocessing and Excel spreadsheet programs in the same package.

Forms and Supplies   Stationery and other printed supplies are tools of the trade to implement written communications for your business. They should be prepared to reflect the image you want to portray, whether it be dignified, dynamic, efficient, flamboyant, or whatever. These paperwork items need not be costly to look professional.

You may or may not have a specially designed logo for your business. If you do have a logo, it should be on each stationery item. In any event, all the stationery items should be designed to match each other. These items include letterhead, envelopes, business cards, labels, and brochures and flyers.

Along with or instead of a logo, some consultants use a motto or a few words describing the business's motto or scope, such as "A Satisfied Client Is Our Mandate" or "Database Management Services."

Stationery

Letterheads are becoming increasingly complex these days. In addition to the traditional information—person's name, title, company name, address, and phone number—you now probably need a fax number, e-mail address, and maybe an Internet web site code.

These features are further complicated in larger firms where the names and numbers of different staff members must be appropriately recorded. These firms must choose between having all the members' names, titles, and numbers on one letterhead; creating a separate letterhead for each member; or doing both. Whatever decision is made, care must be given to the letterhead design to make sure that the abundance of information required is presented clearly.

Business Cards

Business cards are an important tool in the networking process, where the exchange of cards between newly acquainted persons who have found some mutual interest is the first step in establishing a business relationship. Consultants use business cards to make entries in their database of contacts.

The problem with business card design is squeezing all the data required into the limited space available.

Brochures and Flyers

Brochures and flyers are promotional pieces—brochures describing services, credentials, and methods; and flyers covering one-time events or products. Both promotional items should use a printing style and design consistent with those of the other stationery items, and the same logo or motto.

See chapter 5 for two sample brochures.

Labels and Envelopes

Envelopes of the number 10 size (4" x 9 1/2") are a must, and larger sizes may be preprinted with business identification as needed. Labels can be purchased also, for use in mailing packages. All envelopes and labels should have the business's name and address, possibly with a logo or motto added, and with type and design compatible with other stationery items.

Budget and Financial Controls

Budget and financial controls can be relatively simple, with refinements added as they become needed or desirable for analysis purposes. Reviewed here are the basic elements required and features that may prove beneficial in designing financial statements and budget controls, and in applying cost-saving strategies.

Financial Statements

Accounting records need to keep track of expenditures and income, the basic elements of an Income Statement. Assets and liabilities are of less interest and concern for a consulting business. The Income Statement and Balance Sheet are the primary formal financial reports of a business organization.

The minimum record is shown in the Consultant's Financial Spreadsheet on page 000. This can be a manually prepared worksheet. Monthly totals on that spreadsheet show total income and detail expenses by type, as required by the IRS tax form for proprietorships. Expenses are posted to this worksheet by recording each check issued, and income is recorded by posting each receipt.

Other formats for Income Statements are included in accounting software, as are Balance Sheets, which would be suitable for and readily adapted to the needs of any business. If you use an accountant, he or she may suggest some other accounting statement formats or modifications of the software standard designs.

An easy way to keep track of time to be billed to the clients is shown on the following Project Log, used by the Robert B. Fast Associates, Inc.

	DATE	LOCATION	ACTIVITY	HOURS	
1					1
2					2
3					3
4					4
5					5
6					6
7					7
8					8
9					9
10					10
11					11
12					12
13					13
14					14
15					15
16					16
17					17
18					18
19					19
20					20
21					21
22					22
23					23
24					24
25					25
26					26
27					27
28					28
29					29
30					30
31					31
	CLIENT				
	PROJECT				

PROJECT LOG

Budget Controls   A budget is usually thought of in terms of expense control. In most businesses, such as manufacturing and retailing, sales are more or less regular, and budgets are a means of planning and controlling expenses, thereby increasing the margins and profitability.

In consulting, especially independent consulting, expenses are by their nature relatively small, and the factor that has the prime influence on profitability is the sales, or client billings. Therefore, the answer to the question "How are you doing?" depends on your actual income versus projected income.

There are a variety of ways to compare regularly how you expected to do financially with how things actually turn out. One rather simple method is to take an annual financial projection, as discussed in chapter 2 and reproduced on page 139. Add columns to show the actual amounts for each quarter in comparison to the forecasts, as shown on the worksheet Comparison—Actual to Forecast, on page 140.

First-Year Cash Projection

	End of First Quarter	End of Second Quarter	End of Third Quarter	End of Fourth Quarter
Cash - Beginning	30,000	20,400	20,100	20,900
Income:				
Billings		5,000	11,000	14,000
Seminars				1,000
Other				
TOTAL INCOME		5,000	11,000	15,000
Outgo:				
Own salary	5,000	5,000	10,000	15,000
Supplies	500	100	100	100
Travel	100	200	100	200
Other (computer)	4,000			
TOTAL OUTGO	9,600	5,300	10,200	15,300
Cash - End of Qtr.	20,400	20,100	20,900	20,600

Of course, as stated in chapter 2, you would probably wish to show different and possibly more detail in the line items of income and expenses, depending on the nature of your business.

Accounting software packages usually incorporate budget features, and you may find that computerized budget features fit your periodic review and planning processes, with or without modification.

One part of the suggested quarterly financial review is an analysis of expenses, even though the major influence on profitability is income. Some cost saving suggestions follow.

Cost-Saving Ideas   Whether or not costs seem to be the major influence on a consulting business's profitability, it is a good idea to review ways to keep costs in line when analyzing your financial results and plans. Here are a variety of cost-control ideas to keep in mind.

COMPARISON -- ACTUAL TO FORECAST

	End of First Quarter		End of Second Quarter		End of Third Quarter		End of Fourth Quarter	
	Forecast	Actual	Forecast	Actual	Forecast	Actual	Forecast	Actual
Cash - Beginning	30,000		20,400		20,100		20,900	
Income:								
Billings			5,000		11,000		14,000	
Seminars							1,000	
Other								
TOTAL INCOME			5,000		11,000		15,000	
Outgo:								
Own salary	5,000		5,000		10,000		15,000	
Supplies	500		100		100		100	
Travel	100		200		100		200	
Other (computer)	4,000							
TOTAL OUTGO	9,600		5,300		10,200		15,300	
Cash - End of Qtr.	20,400		20,100		20,900		20,600	

- Make your office in your home or, if that is not practical, share an office with another individual practitioner with whom you can share office costs like copiers, fax, and secretarial services.

- Do your own typing and use voice mail to avoid secretarial costs.

- Use tasteful, professional but inexpensive stationery.

- If you need assistance, retain helpers by the hour or day, and bill their costs to a client if feasible.

- Meet prospects in their offices rather than at lunch, which eliminates a cost and gives you a better understanding of your client and the client's environment.

- Use your spouse's medical insurance, if possible. Or, check into insurance plans offered by professional associations.

- Take advantage of free technical periodicals available in your specialties, also free computer hardware and software seminars put on by many vendors.

Areas where it is advisable not to look for savings are your marketing program, computer system, time with potential clients, association and networking activities, and insurance against disasters such as disability, home, and health.

Planning Your Own "Fringe Benefits"

Part of being an independent consultant or practitioner is arranging for insurance and retirement funding. Most major employers have plans available for their employees that cover these personal financial needs. But independent consultants must take care of these needs themselves.

Some associations have insurance benefit plans available for their members at group rates, an important option to look for and take advantage of. The areas reviewed next are medical insurance, errors and omissions insurance, disability insurance, and pension or retirement financial arrangements.

Medical Insurance

The cost of medical care has been increasing dramatically in recent years. Though government and industry pressures seem to be controlling some medical costs, the future is uncertain. The one thing that remains certain, however, is that personal protection from a medical calamity is absolutely essential to avoid the possibility of a personal tragedy.

There are four options for medical insurance: (1) continuing a former employer's arrangement temporarily, on an individual basis, (2) a spouse's family coverage, (3) group coverage through an association, and (4) negotiating an individual policy with an insurance carrier.

According to the Consolidated Omnibus Budget Reconciliation Act (COBRA), employers who have group medical plans are required to offer continuing coverage for terminating employees for a limited period, typically a year and a half. This gives employees time to develop more permanent alternative arrangements.

If you have a spouse whose employer provides group medical coverage for the family, that is likely to be the best possible solution.

Many associations have arrangements for group medical plans for their members, including the Institute of Management Consultants (IMC), the Independent Computer Consultants Association (ICCA), and the National Writers Union.

If other options are not available, the remaining alternative is to secure an individual policy. That is the most expensive option, and if you have a preexisting medical condition, the insurance company might require a waiver for that condition, or might refuse to issue a policy. If the latter occurs, you may be able to get assistance from the state insurance commissioner's office.

Errors and Omissions

Both the Institute of Management Consultants (IMC) and the Independent Computer Consultants Association (ICCA) have arrangements with agents who can provide errors-and-omissions insurance coverage for their members.

Disability

Disability insurance provides for compensation if you are unable to perform your vocation. It is expensive, but important to have to prevent an unlikely but possible disaster. Most policies pay only up to 60 percent of your income so as to avoid providing an incentive for you to declare yourself disabled. Coverage should be arranged for from a grace period after you are disabled up to the time Social Security payments would start.

If at all possible, it is desirable to begin disability coverage before leaving regular employment because payments then can be based on a regular income amount. After an independent consulting business is started, the irregularity of income can make it difficult to establish the income base on which to calculate payments.

Retirement Financing　　Most employers have some pension provisions in their employee benefits programs, along with tax deferred set-asides that help employees provide additional funding for their retirement years.

Independent consultants must make their own provisions for retirement living expenses. In doing so, they should first determine any pension amounts that may be available from previous employers' plans, and also what may be expected from Social Security payments. The balance of retirement living expenses should be paid for through tax deferred set-aside plans that meet IRS requirements. The available plans, whose key provisions are summarized next, are:

Simplified Employee Pension (SEP-IRA)

Keogh—Defined Contribution Plan

Keogh—Defined Benefit Plan

The calculations in weighing these alternatives can be somewhat complex. For further information, see IRS publication 560, "Retirement Plans for the Self-Employed." This is an area where the counsel of an accountant or other advisor may be worthwhile.

Simplified Employee Pension (SEP-IRA). With the SEP-IRA, you can set aside and invest up to 15 percent of pre-tax earnings up to a maximum of $30,000 a year. The funds are not taxed until they are withdrawn. After age $59\frac{1}{2}$ amounts you withdraw are taxed as ordinary income. Amounts withdrawn before $59\frac{1}{2}$ are taxed as income with an added 10 percent penalty. Amounts set aside each year can vary, as long as they are below the maximum.

Keogh—Defined Contribution Plan. There are two types. With a "profit sharing" Defined Contribution Plan, like the SEP-IRA, you may set aside up to 15 percent of earnings, and the amount may vary from year to year. With a "money purchase" Defined Contribution Plan, the set-aside can be up to 25 percent with a maximum of $30,000, but it must be the same amount each year, and the plan must apply evenly to any and all employees. A withdrawal from either type plan may be averaged over five years for tax purposes.

Keogh—Defined Benefit Plan. Under this plan, you define the benefit payments you wish for the plan to provide, then calculate the contributions necessary to produce a fund that can provide those retirement benefits. The Defined Benefit Plan is suitable for those with incomes over $100,000, particularly if they expect to retire in fewer than 10 years. This plan can be made to shelter up to 40 or 50 percent of earnings, but it does require an actuary to do the computations. A withdrawal from the plan may be averaged over five years for tax purposes.

Tax Reports

Accounting records set up for managing a business are generally sufficient for the preparation of tax returns. The records need to show what money came in and went out, and for what purposes expenditures were made. It helps, however, if expense categories are the same as those required by the IRS so that totals can be posted directly to the tax returns without any refiguring.

Proprietorship

The Consultant's Financial Spreadsheet shown earlier is designed with expense headings that correspond to the expense categories required on IRS Schedule C (Form 1040), used for proprietorship returns. However, in a small business these income and expense records could easily be kept by hand on accounting columnar pads. Quicken and other software can provide similar breakdowns, and, of course, it is possible to retain a part-time bookkeeper to do the posting, either manually or by computer.

Proprietorships are also required to submit a Schedule SE, Social Security Self-Employment Tax, along with their Form 1040s, covering their Social Security payments on income earned.

Partnership

Each partnership needs to prepare a Form 1065 showing the partners' earnings. Each partner then reports his or her partnership income on a Schedule K-1, Partner's Share of Income, Credits, Deductions, etc. of Form 1065 and also on Schedule E, Income or Loss from Partnership and S Corporations, submitted with the personal tax return, Form 1040.

The self-employment tax is also shown on Schedule SE, Social Security Self-Employment Tax, which is attached to Form 1040.

Corporation

S corporation earnings are reported along with the personal income tax return, Form 1040. The earnings are reported on Schedule E, Income or Loss from Partnerships and S Corporations, and the self-employment tax is shown on Schedule SE, Social Security Self-Employment Tax.

The C corporation is a separate entity for tax purposes. Therefore, the corporation's profits and taxes must be reported by using Form 1120. Then you report on your personal income tax return, Form 1040, the salary and dividends you have received from the corporation, and the taxes on them, along with any other income.

Estimated Tax Payments

Quarterly payments of your estimated annual tax are required for proprietors, partners, and S corporation owners when the tax amounts are expected to be in excess of $500. Payments should be submitted to the IRS along with Form 1040-ES, Estimated Tax for Individuals.

C corporations also pay quarterly estimated taxes when the year's tax is expected to be $500 or more, using Form 1120, Corporation Estimated Tax.

Employees

If you need to use assistants in your practice, it is far and away the easiest to have them bill you and pay them as subcontractors, giving them form 1099s (Form 1099-MISC, Miscellaneous Income) at the end of the year with copies to the federal and state tax authorities reporting the amounts paid them during the year.

Without getting into the myriad of forms and payment schedules, having employees requires withholding from their pay estimated federal, state, and sometimes local, taxes, Social Security and Medicare. You must also compute and pay federal and state unemployment and disability insurance charges. All of this is in addition to preparing year-end W-2, Wage and Tax Statement forms, reports of gross earnings and deductions for each employee, and preemployment forms assuring compliance with immigration law.

All of these employee paperwork requirements can be a heavy burden on a small firm. Some software can ease the task a bit. Having your accountant do the work can be expensive. Computerized services like ADP (Automatic Data Processing) can do much of the paperwork for a modest fee.

W-2 or 1099?

The Internal Revenue Service has been bringing increasing pressure in recent years to have independent contractors reclassified as employees. Their reasoning is logical and clear: if the federal government has an employer send withholding taxes, Social Security, and Medicare before an employee gets them, the IRS is more likely to get payments, and they will get them faster.

The mechanics involve two familar forms, 1099 for a contractor and W-2 for an employee. Contractors or subcontractors who receive more than $600 in a year must receive 1099s from their clients by the following January 31 stating the total amount of such payments. Employees at the time of employment fill out a W-4 form stating their dependents, then receive from their employers by January 31 the W-2 form stating the prior year's gross wages and Social Security, Medicare, and state and local tax deductions. Copies of both forms are sent to the IRS which, of course, compares them to the data on contractors' and employees' income tax returns. But the W-4 form authorizes the employer to forward the deducted estimated tax amounts promptly after they are withheld.

Most consultants who work independently for several clients should expect little problem. But it does affect the method of taking on added help when needed. It is clearly the simplest for a consultant to retain assistants as subcontractors rather than employees, when added staff is required for peak loads or for an expanding business. But if the assistant works on a continuing basis, it may be necessary to shift the arrangement to an employee basis.

The IRS's principal challenges to contract status have been with computer consultants working through brokers, especially on longer term assignments. Although the IRS has a long list of criteria for deciding whether a consultant is an employee or contractor, most of the determining factors are subjective.

An independent consultant whose practice meets these conditions should have little difficulty:

- You serve several clients in the same period.
- You have an established place of business with an investment in operating facilities, even if this office is in your home.
- You do work at your office facility as well as at the clients' venues.
- You have written agreements or contracts with your clients to provide specified services and results.
- You have a business name, either an incorporated name or other firm name.

Checklist   The following checklist will help you review the issues in this chapter as they relate to your consulting plans or practice.

	Yes	No
Has the accounting, tax, legal, and computer advice you obtained proven worth its cost?		
If your business has a computer, have you found it an essential tool, or at least worth the time and cost it involves?		
Are there further computer applications that you are working to implement which appear will benefit the business?		
Do your forms and supplies reflect the image you wish to project for your business?		
Do the financial records and reports give you the information you need to manage the business?		
Have you made financial projections for your business?		
Have you regularly compared actual financial results with earlier financial forecasts?		
Have you evaluated possible methods for reducing costs without impairing the effectiveness of the business?		
Do you have a satisfactory plan for medical insurance?		
Do you have a satisfactory plan for financing your retirement?		
Do you have errors-and-omissions insurance?		
Do you have disability insurance?		

APPENDIX A:
Six Exemplary
Careers

This appendix describes six different and highly successful independent consulting businesses: how they were started and developed, and the personalities, skills, and technologies behind each one. These case examples cover the distinguishing principles on which each business is based, its chronological development, and key lessons to be learned from each one. Some examples include a description of a particularly successful or satisfying client engagement.

The six independent consultant careers described below are entirely different as to the services furnished and the individuals' style and approach. But all of these consultants have a valuable, special knowledge and skill to sell, and a persistence to make a go of their business. These six are:

> Bob Fast of Robert B. Fast Associates, Inc., an expert in developing food products and production processes
>
> Bill Weber of Edge Development Group, Inc., an international business consulting firm
>
> Ray Rauth of RR Enterprises, a leader in planning and designing computer systems for publishing companies

Larry Bassett of The Bassett Consulting Group, Inc., which provides management improvements via a wide range of approaches such as team building, executive coaching, and re-engineering

Fredrica Levinson of FSL Human Resource Services, "a consulting and training firm that specializes in helping organizations develop their people and increase productivity"

Carol Brown of Williams, Brown & Co., Inc., who designed computer systems for and counsels leading clubs in New York City

■ ■ ■ ■

Robert B. Fast Associates, Inc.

Profile—Bob Fast

Bob Fast has had a remarkable and unusual career. He worked 34 years for Nabisco, starting as a junior chemist and rising steadily to the head of process development for grocery products. Having achieved a comfortable financial position, Bob decided to retire at the age of 55, build a retirement home in Vermont, and enjoy his hobbies of fishing, hiking, golfing, and building rustic furniture.

But when it came time to retire, he realized that his knowledge and skills could be of great value to others, and that his temperament was inconsistent with a leisurely lifestyle. So he offered his services gratis to the professional association in his field. The result has been that he has since become extremely busy, and rewarded financially, putting together a textbook about his specialty, conducting short courses in his field, and performing consulting work for companies who need assistance in his areas of expertise. His consulting engagements have involved the development of food-processing methods, often with the assistance of other technicians he knows when related skills and talent are required for the job.

While Bob enjoyed the kind of success that most people dream about in his first career, his second career has provided him with even greater satisfaction. As a consultant he has been invited to give his guidance to food companies as well as to newcomers in the field. Along with other experts, he has compiled a pioneer textbook on breakfast cereal processing. And his peers hold him in high regard as a leader in his field.

His consulting work involves extensive travel, which he

likes, he still has time to devote to his avocations, and he has been able to live in the rural community he and his wife enjoy. And all of his professional activities have provided income he had not expected before he retired.

Bob also gets personal satisfaction from having explained to people in other parts of the world how they can achieve better nutrition economically by using food-processing methods developed in America.

Guiding Principles

A main philosophy of Bob's is always to be totally honorable. He will never undertake a job beyond his own experience and skill, and has referred many inquiries to others because he is well acquainted with the abilities of technicians in areas related to his.

A corollary is, don't procrastinate. Get right to the task you have committed to undertake, and stay with it until it is done. Your reliability in the eyes of your client depends on doing your job on time.

One method that helps Bob meet his scheduled commitments is also a useful tool in his billing and accounting. He maintains a log of his work, both that done at home and at the client's site. This log has columns for date, where the work is performed, description of the activity, and the time spent in tenths of an hour. The log also records toll telephone calls and unusual expenses, e.g., express mail, not regular mail. Bob bills clients for time and expenses, by the day at their premises, by the hour at his home.

Bob's corporate accounting is simple. His den is his office, and his home expenses are prorated to the business on the ratio of the den's square footage to the total house. This ratio applies to fuel, electric bills, and homeowner's insurance.

His main marketing effort has been at the annual technical meetings of the American Association of Cereal Chemists, which has published his book and sponsored his short courses. There he mingles with the members and makes available his brochure (shown in chapter 5) and a five-page curriculum vitae covering details of his education, positions at Nabisco, six patents, professional memberships, publications, and other related data. He is considering mailings to some of the students who have taken his courses over the last five years.

He did pay a significant sum to a publisher of a consultant listing, promoted as a source of consulting leads. The results were zero. Bob cautions others to beware of such schemes.

Bob is listed with Expert Resources Inc.® (for details and a copy of an Expert Resources Inc.® brochure, see chapter 5) which got him one nibble but no money-paying job yet. It costs nothing to be listed by this organization, but they take a percentage of the revenue from any engagement they produce.

Career Steps

After graduating from The Pennsylvania State University in 1951 with a B.S. degree in agricultural and biological chemistry, Bob went right to work for the National Biscuit Co. (now Nabisco). He stayed there until he retired in 1984 except for two years spent in the army as a meat and dairy products inspector. At Nabisco he moved up from entry-level assistant research chemist, to group leader, new product development manager, assistant director of research, and then director of process development for Nabisco's grocery products division.

His work at Nabisco included research, product development, process development, and plant start-up activities. These functions were applied in the such fields as cereal grain milling, dough mixing, snack extrusion and toasting, and breakfast cereal processing. The patents and inventions he developed alone or with others covered innovations such as a continuous process for cooking cereal grains, sugar coating of cereals, and a cereal puffing apparatus.

During this time Bob conducted lectures on cereal technology for Rutgers University and for the Cereal Institute, Inc., and wrote articles on breakfast cereals for *Cereal Science Today* and for *Cereal Foods World*. While with Nabisco, Bob also spent three years on the dietary fiber committee of the American Association of Cereal Chemists, and 16 years on the technical committee of the Cereal Institute, Inc.

As his planned retirement approached, Bob and his wife looked forward to moving to Vermont and bought a lot near where his wife had gone to college. But as his retirement day approached, Bob realized he "did not want his brain go to mush," as he says. He did not want his knowledge to go to waste and wanted to share it. Six weeks before he was to retire, he got in touch with the executive director of the American Association of Cereal Chemists (AACC) and offered his services to the association on a volunteer basis.

About two months after he retired, Bob received a very

nice letter from the executive director asking if he would be willing to help write and co-edit a book on breakfast cereal manufacturing. The association had for some time been trying to get the head of the University of Minnesota's nutrition and food science department to write the book, but he had declined because of the time demands of the project. So Bob's offer overcame the professor's time obstacle, and the two made a good match because their experience dovetailed well to cover the total subject matter of the book. Bob's co-editor, Dr. Elwood F. Caldwell, had spent 20 years at Quaker Oats before joining the University of Minnesota and knew well the hot cereal and nutrition aspects, balancing Bob's cold cereal and industrial processes expertise.

The book, *Breakfast Cereals and How They Are Made*, was published by the American Association of Cereal Chemists in 1990. There were 19 authors altogether, and Bob wrote or co-wrote four of the chapters. The book is a textbook of the basics in the cereals processing industry: how the food ingredients are processed, the machinery used to produce the end products, and related topics like nutritional aspects, flavorings, and packaging. This was the first book on the subject, and it became a key reference for people new to the industry and for those on its fringes who wanted to learn more about specific aspects of breakfast cereals. Of course each cereal manufacturer carefully guards its trade secrets, so the book's contents were confined to information in the public domain, which did not interfere with the book's purpose of thoroughly covering the basic principles, methods, and equipment involved.

Putting together the book required contacting many contributors with diverse expertise and the abilities and willingness to write about their specialties. The co-editors had to coordinate the efforts of the 19 authors to make sure the pieces fit together and that the information was both correct and clearly stated. It helped that vendors often were both knowledgeable and willing. Bob Fast and Elwood Caldwell, fortunately, enjoyed working with each other as the co-leaders of this pioneering book project. The book is now in its third printing. Over 2,500 copies have sold, the publisher's second largest sales volume of any of its books.

After the book was published, the American Association of Cereal Chemists asked Bob if he would direct a short course based on the book. Bob and Elwood developed the course, which continues to be given in the United States annually. It has been conducted nine times with a total of about 300 attendees.

Bob has also been asked to plan two plant facilities for the production of cereal food products. One was for a food-processing company in Japan, which asked for a layout for a cornflake line. (Cereal foods in Japan are mostly sold as snack foods.) The job took 180 worker-days over a period of a year, 1989–1990. To meet the client's requirements, Bob put together a three-member team engaging two other associates—a professional engineer and an accountant—to construct a related manufacturing cost system. In this case, Bob organized an unusual cooperative arrangement. Although he coordinated the work of the three specialists, team members billed the client separately for their own time and expenses.

This engagement was a challenge—an enjoyable, constructive, collaborative effort, putting together from scratch equipment specifications, a layout, and a cost system for a proposed new process. However, the client did not implement their proposal. The client was persuaded by an English firm to buy and install another line of equipment. As it turned out, the English firm's equipment could not meet the client's time and capacity requirements, and so the client came back to Bob for his advice on how to overcome the obstacles arising from this unfortunate decision. The work was all done in the United States. The client paid a reasonable fee for the work, and learned too late the real value of the job Bob and his friends had done.

A year later, Bob fulfilled an additional request for a layout. This was for a bakery pilot plant, and it was done for the Northwest Wheat Commission. Bob spent about 30 days on this engagement, including an on-site visit at Northwest's Portland, Oregon facility.

Both consulting engagements came through referrals from the American Association of Cereal Chemists.

In 1989 Bob was asked to join a five-member group heading to Moscow to lecture at a symposium for eastern block grain scientists. The sponsor of the symposium was the U.S. Wheat Associates, an organization that markets United States wheat overseas. This organization operates in two ways: their twenty offices throughout the world are staffed with marketing and technical people, promoting the purchase of wheat from our country; and their technicians coordinate the resolution of problems and questions that arise from use of wheat purchased from our country.

Other speakers at this Moscow symposium gave lectures on topics such as frozen dough technology and flour milling. Bob's job was to explain how to make a wheat flake. The Russian government was interested in improving their citizens' diet. The typical eastern European breakfast is dry meat—like salami without the garlic—cheese, bread, and coffee. They realized that cereals were one avenue to help achieve their nutrition improvement goals, in addition to benefitting from the economy and convenience of dry cereals.

Bob is taking on another international educational effort by preparing a second edition of his book. This new edition will incorporate technical changes, proprietary information which has recently come into the public domain, and international aspects of cereal product manufacturing. The first edition was limited in scope to United States operations, but conducting the short courses of the American Association of Cereal Chemists in other countries has dramatized the need for broadening the books' scope to include activities and interests in breakfast cereals in other parts of the world. Until recently, breakfast cereals were used only in English speaking countries. Their consumption in other regions of the world is beginning to grow, and so the spreading of learning and knowledge about breakfast cereal technology via the association's book and courses should be of great value in paving the way for worldwide expansion.

Points to Remember

Consulting as a second career can sometimes be even more rewarding than a highly successful first career.

An offer of voluntary services can result in enjoyable and lucrative activities that can even produce social benefits.

Honesty is a main requirement for maintaining a positive reputation, and a positive reputation is a main requirement for achieving future business.

Important Engagement

Bob's most important client has been the American Association of Cereal Chemists. They asked him to co-edit the book they published and sponsored the short courses he has conducted worldwide. These activities have taken a major part of his time during his second consulting career. And, of course, these activities have helped him generate the reputation and contacts which have produced other consulting business.

The main rewarding engagement of the more traditional sort, i.e., a commercial client with a problem to solve, was his undertaking for the Japanese food manufacturer. This project was satisfying because it had a well-defined objective, the objective was well within the capabilities of the project team, their work was professionally done, and they were all well and promptly paid. The one disappointing drawback, of course, was the fact that the client did not carry out their recommendations.

■   ■   ■   ■

Edge Development Group, Inc.
Profile–Bill Weber

Edge Development Group, Inc. ("EDG") is a small enterprise specializing in top-level counsel and guidance to governments and businesses, primarily in the international arena. The firm is "dedicated to practical recommendations and to the competitive success of clients." EDG focuses on helping governments and private sector companies exploit international business opportunities.

The group is headed by William D. Weber and his wife Betsy, who are supported by other executive specialists as required by the engagements underway, up to 13 persons in the past. Founded in 1976 in Dubai, in the United Arab Emirates (UAE), the firm moved its headquarters via London to the United States in 1985. It is currently managed from the firm's headquarters in the Webers' home in Ridgefield, Connecticut.

The firm's initial clients were primarily in the Arabian Gulf Region, where Bill had been brought up when his father was an executive in Aramco. Over time, their client base has expanded to many other parts of the world.

Guiding Principles

In our discussions about his firm's success and how it has been achieved, Bill explained some of his operating philosophies. The key, to him, is a two-part requirement: You must develop (1) a reputation for achieving worthwhile practical results and (2) trust. Reputation building, of course, depends on actually achieving beneficial results for your clients and on letting that news be spread by word of mouth and other means. Trust, like the reputation, takes time to develop. Usually that comes with a long-term relationship, or from reassurances from mutual acquaintances. Trust means that clients know that your efforts will be to further their best interests, that information will be kept confidential, and that your word is reliable—that you can be counted on to do what you say you will do, and that you are scrupulously honest.

Bill emphasized reputation as the key this way: "If the principal element in your business development strategy is not reputation, then you probably should be in another business." And he added that most of EDG's client engagements have started after somebody made a recommendation.

In his early days as an independent consultant, Bill worked hard to build a reputation and trust among Arab potential clients. Knowing something of the Arabian culture and language and having spent considerable time working and living with the Arab people, he was accepted fairly quickly as a professional who could offer assistance to Arab business people. They came to value Bill's knowledge of American ways of doing business in addition to his management skills. This acceptance grew in spite of the fact that, in Arab culture and experience at that stage, there was virtually no tradition of sharing proprietary business information with outside business professionals.

Because reputation is so essential to consulting success, it is important to avoid mistakes, which could damage your reputation. However, too much caution is also unwise, as boldness is often of value. A balance here is important, for which sound judgment is a requisite.

Bill noted in passing that the recent opening up of free enterprise in eastern Europe has created a deluge of people seeking easy profits from the shift from Communism to free enterprise. A certain number of charlatans, calling themselves consultants, have damaged the reputation of the consulting profession in general. That has made it difficult for reliable professionals in the field to overcome a broadly unfavorable image as they attempt to develop prospective clients in eastern Europe—a situation somewhat similar to that in Arabia in the seventies, when Bill was getting started there.

Regarding the internal management of the business, Bill discussed several operating guidelines that he has found helpful and tries to follow.

- Stay small, so as to be easily manageable; EDG's top size has been thirteen people, but the present seven or less is optimum for his view of comfort.

- Because a staff member may be working independently thousands of miles away, effective communication is critical. Bill, Betsy, and project team leaders make frequent visits and reviews; a spirit of teamwork is fundamental. The so-called "doctrine of no surprises" is very important.

- All staff members continually preach about, and practice, good listening skills; a client's needs must be heard and understood if they are to be addressed and resolved.

- Bill and Betsy are not at all shy about finding staff people who are "smarter than we are" or who have skills and experience beyond their own; job performance and the firm's reputation are usually enhanced thereby.

- Work and travel schedules are created with ample time allotments so that commitments can be undertaken with rested minds. "You owe at least that to each client."

- What Bill calls "administrivia"—tasks such as accounting and scheduling—must be done efficiently so they don't interfere with client services and business development activities. So Bill finds that "administrivia" is sometimes addressed evenings and weekends.

- Engagement management and business development must always be properly balanced.

- Clients often are paying for perspective, and it's important to keep that in mind throughout the development of client relationships.

- While people on staff may do much of the work with clients, you must continue to do hands-on work. Both clients and the professional staff have every right to expect that.

The firm's write-up for potential clients lists the following operating principles:

- Systematic quality control is an essential element in all of our work.

- Objectivity and disciplined analytical practices are important elements of the value of our work for our clients.

- Effective and continuous communication between ourselves and each client is essential to the success of our work.

- Confidentiality is critically important to our clients.

- Conflicts of interest must be avoided.

- Political consulting, *per se*, is not our field.

- Practicality is a critical and consistent element of our professional practice, of our reputation, and of our success.

Career Steps   After graduating from Yale in 1960, Bill joined a large, publicly held corporation that was not especially well managed. With his vigor and ambition, he enjoyed fairly rapid advancement in the management ranks of that company. After a few years, he was asked by its management to represent the corporation in an established joint venture co-owned with another company. The venture was a primary aluminum producer in which the two companies were absentee partners. Each partner used metal offtake from the venture to support industrial product fabrication operations. As the resident representative of one of the partner investors, Bill had to deal with difficult management problems that sorely needed to be remedied, including a union which had achieved undue power, demoralized supervision, absence of management controls, poor safety performance, inadequate quality control, inadequate cost control, and inadequate data for use in attacking these problems. Bill instituted many improvements which lessened some of the problems, but was prevented from real progress by the structure of the ownership. His proposal to sell the venture put him in disfavor.

So, after almost ten years in corporate management positions, he decided to move on because he did not have the power to properly fulfill his responsibilities. He accepted a position as a staff consultant with McKinsey & Company, Inc., a leading management consulting firm. McKinsey was seeking people with hands-on managerial experience for their consulting staff. That new position provided relief from his frustrations, and excitement and stimulation from the brilliance and talent of the McKinsey members he was to work with. He had been with a team that was undistinguished, and now was with a team in which he had to sprint to keep up. The consulting profession, especially the challenge of working with some of the leading practitioners in that field, was an exciting revelation to Bill.

After four years with McKinsey, Bill and Betsy had some long discussions about where they wanted to go and how to get there. In spite of the value of being with an outstanding firm, some of the demands seriously conflicted with family life. Staff members at McKinsey frequently worked weekends, canceled vacations, and otherwise sacrificed personal matters for the welfare of the firm. He observed some of his peers becoming workaholics in their efforts to meet internal competitive pressures, with damaging family consequences.

Bill had suggested that McKinsey expand into the Middle East where he felt there was a market for consulting and where his own experience could be helpful. However, McKinsey in the early seventies seemed satisfied with its other successes and showed little interest in Bill's proposal.

While weighing career opportunities, a fortunate offer came Bill's way. The head of a consulting firm in Beirut, Lebanon, asked him to come aboard as he needed another American on his staff. The head of this firm, Mideast Industrial Relations Counselors, Inc. (MEIRC), an extremely intelligent and well-educated Palestinian, had worked for Bill's father when his father was an executive for Aramco.

MEIRC's clients were mostly in, or related to, the oil business, and the work in organization and human resource management was interesting. But soon Beirut became dangerous and intolerable (in 1975 and 1976), so MEIRC decided to move to Athens.

Rather than make that change, Bill and Betsy decided to go it alone and, through the contacts they had made, began consulting work on the eastern edge of the Arab Peninsula. They made their headquarters in Dubai and developed engagements with oil companies, offering a broad range of organizational, manpower management, and operational consulting. Their firm, Middle East Management Services, Inc. (MEMSI) was formally established in 1976 under a charter granted by Sheik Rashid bin Said al Maktoum, the Ruler of Dubai and Vice President of UAE. Clientele grew to include government agencies, multinational corporations, and indigenous Arab companies in the Gulf region.

They got very much involved in the processes of nationalization of the producing oil companies in the Gulf Region. The nationalization transition involved changing relationships and operating methods among the players: the various operating companies in each country; the "parent companies" in Europe, North America, and Asia; and the emerging petroleum ministries in each country. This transition created consulting opportunities in a wide range of organizational and operating areas, which Bill and his firm were well able to provide. For example, using a holding company as the organizational basis for integrating and managing the disparate operations of a national oil company was virtually unprecedented in Arabia in the mid-seventies—when the need for such an organizational form was becoming urgent.

In 1984 Bill and his wife moved their business headquarters, in stages, back to the United States. They went first to London for a short period, then to Manhattan, and finally to Connecticut, where they have been for the past ten years. The Webers like living in a nonurban atmosphere and have found that Connecticut is a practical base for an international business. Travel is always required, but any location can serve as a base, and Connecticut satisfies their personal tastes and interests. When they repatriated their firm to the U.S., they renamed it Edge Development Group, Inc.

Following are highlights of some EDG engagements on behalf of foreign government clients:

> Assisted the government of Dubai, in the United Arab Emirates, in evaluating its economic development assets and enhancing its attractiveness as a magnet for direct corporate investments from the United States, Europe, and Japan.

> Assisted the Central Bank of the Republic of Cyprus in adjusting regulatory and communications practices so as to enhance that country's competitiveness as a regional business center; then designed and carried out a working program that resulted in establishment of seven new U.S. corporate offices in Cyprus in the initial year.

> Formulated an international economic development plan for the City of Paris and the surrounding Ile-de-France Region of France, and then implemented an ongoing marketing program to generate substantial direct investment into the region from U.S. corporations. To date, as a direct result of this undertaking, Ile-de-France has benefitted from some 50 new U.S. business ventures in the region involving close to a thousand new jobs.

> Developed strategies to attract foreign investment for state-owned enterprises and regional authorities in France and the United Kingdom, supported by related marketing programs in the United States.

And following are synopses of some of EDG's engagements on behalf of corporations and other private sector clients:

> Designed and directed organizational and multinational staffing plans to support construction and then stable operation of a $2 billion aluminum smelter in Arabia.

> Assisted in establishing the holding company concept as the basis for reorganizing the Abu Dubai National Oil Company.

Developed business diversification plans for the largest airport and air travel organization in the Arabian Gulf Region, to help it respond successfully to changing competitive and political conditions.

Assisted a Kuwaiti family in organizing its diverse and substantial international business interests. Convinced the family members, who lacked formal business training, of the practical value of disciplined management practices. Helped them to institute effective management practices while maintaining established cultural traditions.

Defined an effective U.S. market entry strategy for a large French manufacturer of medical products.

Developed Eldercare, a system for dependable delivery of nonmedical personal support services to elderly people living at home in the U.S.

The staffing of the Edge Development Group has varied with the demands of the engagements at hand. Thirteen has been the maximum number. Their ideal size is four or five professional people. These generally have included a financial person, who is skilled in computers and systems, and a contract administrator. Others are professional consultants capable of fulfilling the needs and expectations of the clients. These staff members have been mostly subcontractors, allowing for flexibility to meet the changing mix of client activity. However, because typical assignments extend over a year or two, and often involve some years of follow-up work, staff turnover has been relatively low.

Typically, either Bill or Betsy Weber negotiates any engagement with a new client and one of them follows its progress closely. That means fairly frequent visits and reviews with the client and staff involved.

Points to Remember

A main requirement for success is to establish and maintain a reputation for producing beneficial practical results for your clients, and for being honest and reliable in your dealings with them.

In establishing a new business, look to your experience for any unique qualities that can be of value to clients. Bill Weber gained a competitive edge by establishing a niche for himself at the beginning, based on his familiarity with Arab culture and tradition plus his top-level American business and consulting experience.

Important
Engagements

EDG has provided the following two brief summaries of (1) an especially important assignment in the private sector part of their practice and (2) a similarly notable piece of work in the public sector.

Private Sector. An oil company in the Arabian Gulf had been managed for decades as essentially just another unit of its parent company, which is based in the U.S. The culture and operating standards of the Western managers and supervisors who were periodically rotated through this foreign operation reflected the culture and operating standards expected and rewarded in the oil industry in the southwestern U.S. By the mid-seventies, those southwestern U.S. values were clearly out of step with emerging local and regional pride and capabilities. Arab managers and technocrats were emerging as powerful and effective leaders in the petroleum industry in their region. And of course the rulers of the region had long since clarified any lingering questions as to who owned the hydrocarbon reserves under their land.

At this stage, the parent company made an unusual and fortuitous choice in replacing the retiring head of the local operation. They sent a man who had sophisticated international business background in both Europe and the Middle East. In fact, the new president had been directly involved in the establishment of the local operation many years earlier.

He saw immediately the conflict between parent company values and emerging local conditions and, more important, he saw the operational damage that had so far resulted. He was determined to reverse a deteriorating situation.

Based on his knowledge of EDG's activities in the region, he asked EDG to work with him on his transition into his new job. Fairly quickly, however, both saw the need for fundamental recasting of virtually all aspects of human resource management in the local company. They agreed that instituting changes in this broad area of management could be an effective way to intervene in the generally deteriorating operating performance and to replace inappropriate established practices with more effective ways to do business.

Over a period of some 30 months, working mainly with the local management, EDG improved parent company selection criteria for managerial and supervisory staff assigned to the Arab operation. EDG instituted staff planning, training, and development programs to better utilize both national and non-national Arabs in the company. They established pay practices that are externally competitive, internally equitable, and directly related to individual performance levels. And EDG accomplished these changes in ways that were eventually understood and supported by the parent company management.

Operational performance, including productivity and safety, improved as a result of these changes. And relations with the local government were stabilized in ways that have proved valuable to all parties.

Public Sector. In the late seventies, EDG began consciously to develop a professional practice targeted at helping local, regional, and national governments to define and implement effective international economic development strategies—usually with the specific goal of attracting direct corporate investment. EDG developed this part of their practice while helping the Government of Dubai formulate a diversification strategy to broaden their economic base beyond the petroleum sector. Subsequent activity in this field, mainly serving European clients, has been varied and quite extensive.

As a direct result of their growing reputation for effectiveness in this extremely competitive field, they were asked in 1990 to represent in the U.S. the economic development interests of the capital region of France, the Paris/Ile-de-France Region. They have subsequently been directly involved in the establishment in Ile-de-France of numerous new business activities by American-based corporations, resulting in hundreds of new jobs.

Recently, as a result of their work for Ile-de-France, one of the world's truly distinguished technology companies decided to establish a global research development facility in Ile-de-France. That decision represents an investment of $100 million and the creation of hundreds of high-skilled new jobs. Competition from other regions was strong. EDG's role in the negotiations leading to this important strategic decision was critical to the outcome and demonstrates their effectiveness in the international economic development.

At the outset, Ile-de-France competed with five other regions of France; with several locations in the United Kingdom; and, at various stages in the negotiations, with sites in Ireland, Belgium, the Netherlands, Spain, and Italy. Within six to eight months, the choice of location was narrowed to France, Ireland, and Glasgow.

Of the locations in France, Ile-de-France was the strongest candidate because of the large number of R&D facilities already located there. The U.S. company wanted its new lab to be able to undertake joint research with other prominent institutions.

Scotland and Ireland remained viable alternatives throughout the negotiations, at least partially because both were able to offer greater financial incentives than could be granted from the aggregate of all three levels of government involved in the discussions on behalf of Ile-de-France.

EDG was an active participant in the data gathering and analysis that formed the basis for this initial distillation of the possible choices.

Through a lengthy series of meetings and telephone conversations, EDG developed a close working relationship with the American-based senior corporate decision-maker for the project, a vice president and director of the company. One of this executive's responsibilities was to ensure that the R&D project would receive as much support as possible from authorities at national, regional, and local levels—both initially and for many years to come.

Concurrently, the economic development agency for Ile-de-France, the immediate client, was able to develop an effective working relationship with the company's senior executive in France, who would direct the project if it were sited anywhere in France. The company's president for Europe also became an important participant toward the end of the negotiations.

These separate but parallel sets of working relationships, developed over the course of the negotiations, were crucial to the successful outcome. EDG and the client agency were able to compare reactions and to gain feedback from both U.S. and European executives at each step in the process. Detailed documentation by EDG describing and analyzing the company's evolving corporate positions helped the client because it communicated to the appropriate authorities in France the obstacles that needed to be overcome in order to move the project forward. Similarly, the client's proposed solutions to various obstacles were "suggested" at the corporate level by EDG in order to gain corporate reaction before incorporating those elements into formal commitments by the agency or by any of the other negotiating principals in Ile-de-France.

Most important, these relationships were critical in keeping the negotiation process on track. In several instances, when politics interfered—as is common in high profile projects—EDG was able to determine what had transpired and to inform the client. The client could then take appropriate action to counter political pressures introduced in the hope of steering the decision toward a competing location.

EDG's involvement in the project began in November 1994. The decision to locate the new R&D Center in Ile-de-France was announced in February 1996—a relatively short time span for a decision on a high profile project of this magnitude.

■ ■ ■ ■

RR Enterprises

Profile—Ray Rauth

RR Enterprises is the name Ray Rauth uses for his computer systems consulting business. Ray has developed a niche in which he is a top expert, and he has a lifestyle that is very satisfying to him. For a dozen years a major part of his business has been developing and installing computer systems for the publishing industry. He enjoys working on his own as a solo independent, living in a wooded area of a lovely, rural town in Connecticut, and commuting once a week or so to his clients in New York City. But he maintains a large network of contacts in the computer and consulting fields, having been a founder of a local chapter of the Independent Computer Consultants Association, and moving up from there to become president and currently chairman of the international association.

Guiding Principles

Staying small has been a carefully considered plan. As his reputation grew in his specialized field, and the demand for his services increased, Ray deliberated at some length about launching an expansion plan. Some of his analysis was done during his frequent runs in the countryside near his home (he is an avid marathon runner), a time he finds fosters thinking through such issues. He concluded that becoming a business manager with several employees or subcontractors would be more hectic and less satisfying to his personal tastes and temperament than working alone. So he remains an independent, using subcontractors only occasionally when needed for a peak workload or a particular technical specialty.

Ray says that you have to define in your own mind what you mean by success. If you are in business for yourself, you can do anything you make your mind up to do, with suitable determination. He feels he has found true success by achieving the quality of life he desires.

Independent consulting involves the kind of interpersonal relationships that Ray likes best. Talking with clients about their needs and making a software system to fulfill those needs are things Ray enjoys doing. But having someone supervise his work on a daily basis is definitely not his cup of tea.

But because he is a solo practitioner, the business is always present. For example, Ray recently went to bed with an unsolved problem on his mind and drowsed off thinking about it. On waking the next morning, the solution, which had eluded him the day before, seemed quite clear—an experience he feels occurs with many independent business people.

Ray considers consulting a fine solution to the downsizing epidemic for computer specialists. Two acquaintances of his were dropped by IBM a while ago. One has become a successful consultant, now heading a sizable business with several employees. The other, to whom Ray subcontracted some work, tried consulting for a while with modest success, but felt uncomfortable without a regular paycheck. He then joined Microsoft, and is now one of its 2,000 millionaire employees. There are several ex-IBMers in Ray's chapter of the Independent Computer Consultants Association.

Career Steps   Prior to launching his independent consulting practice a dozen years ago, Ray Rauth spent a few years in the military and NASA, then over a decade as a university faculty member. Teaching and training continue to be a small part of his business.

After receiving his BS in mathematics at the University of Arkansas in 1962, Ray was a lieutenant in the USAF for four years with various electronics and training duties. Then he was an engineer for NASA for another four years.

He started as a part-time student in 1970 at Baruch University, where he earned his MBA. But he also worked there until 1982, first as a research assistant at their academic computer center and ultimately as the associate director of that center. At Baruch he also taught as an adjunct lecturer in both degree and certificate programs.

Ray left Baruch in 1982 to become executive vice president of a new training and consulting firm. Some investors in that venture were his first clients when he left that firm to launch his own individual practice. After working for them for six months or so on a full-time engagement, Ray received a consulting assignment from another client. He then shortened the time he spent on his first engagement, and raised his rates. He was off and running as a solo computer consultant.

Shortly thereafter, through a friend of his who was managing editor for a major publishing company, Ray began computer development work that paved the way for what has become the main thrust of his work for the last decade. Since then he has designed and installed publishing computer systems for functions like book planning and scheduling, inventory control, and marketing. A major client has been Simon and Schuster, along with its many divisions and departments, like Prentice-Hall.

There has been a beneficial synergy in this publishing industry specialization because the publication process is similar from one company to the next. Therefore, the system design for each company does not require reinventing the wheel all over again, because many of the features of the earlier designs may be carried over to new projects. This synergy has given Ray a competitive edge which has helped him carve out and maintain a respected position in the publishing industry.

Part of Ray's success in the publishing field has been his judicious handling of copyrights for the systems he has designed. In some cases he has applied for copyrights by applying to the Library of Congress. However, copyrights are legally protectable by keeping evidence of the time and substance of a system's creation. His agreements with his clients give the clients perpetual use of the systems he creates for them, and authorize them to modify and maintain the systems themselves. But, at the same time, the clients' use is limited; if a client acquires another group of publishing companies, the client is not authorized to use Ray's systems in the new firms without negotiating a compensation arrangement with Ray, the copyright owner.

Usually, with a new client Ray prepares a specification document stating the work to be done and compensation terms. With larger projects, these documents may require lawyers for each party and formal legal contracts. However, with existing clients, continuing work usually begins when clients say they need a certain change. They discuss it a bit; then Ray confirms in a note what he intends to do and how.

As to reports to the client, on some projects Ray does a regular weekly report. On other projects, he'll give a report only when appropriate or when there is a special need. For example, if a problem occurs, Ray will usually report that in writing to make sure the client is properly alerted. On new computer systems, he gives the client a technical write-up and the source code. In some cases, his engagement specifies that he will provide user procedure documentation.

While he subcontracts work during peak periods, he also accepts assignments from a broker when his workload permits. He finds working via a broker quite satisfactory, but of course he much prefers working directly with the client in defining and fulfilling the job.

Ray has never had to launch any sizable marketing campaign to secure business. His reputation in the publishing field and his contacts via the Independent Computer Consultants Association have sufficed to give his business the momentum that it needs. He has never prepared a flyer or brochure covering his experience and fields of expertise.

He did place a series of ads in a local paper for two or three years just to see if it might be worthwhile. He got in return tire kickers who were obviously checking out what someone else told them, two people who wanted to work for him, and one or two who wanted to sell him some computer equipment. His conclusion: ads don't pay off for consulting work.

Ray does suggest computer on-line services as a way of exploring new business opportunities, though he has not gotten business referrals from them himself. Consult forums are a way to develop dialogs between people with common interests. There is always the possibility that such discussions might end up uncovering a match between a capability and a need. Besides, the cost is modest, and the conversations are sometimes fun, sometimes illuminating.

Ray has never found a need to document his business plan. But he has always had a plan clearly developed in his mind of where he wanted to go and how to get there. His plan often is expanded and modified as experience and opportunities warrant, but is never written. However, Ray does advise new consultants to have a definite and clear concept of what they plan to do, and he urges that the plan should be written if more than one person is involved. In any case, the plan needs to be thoroughly thought through.

Throughout his career, Ray has continued his teaching and training activities, which help polish the skills and image needed for consulting. They also provide an income source that can even out some of the consulting irregularities. His activities have included adjunct teaching assignments at New York University, Long Island University, the Grad Center of the City University of New York, and occasional corporate training sessions.

Points to Remember

One excellent route to a successful independent consultancy is via developing a niche, a specialty in which you know as much as or more than any other expert in the field.

It pays to be flexible, and to take advantage of opportunities that present themselves. Ray's first publishing engagement revealed to him an absence of good computer systems in the publishing field. He has been a prime mover in filling that gap, and thereby became a formidable specialist in the publishing industry computer systems niche.

Creating a business that matches your lifestyle can be more satisfying and enjoyable than making a bundle by growing into a big enterprise.

Being a leader in a professional association can help establish your reputation as a leader in the specialty of your consulting business.

Ads can be a waste of time and money as a source of leads for consulting projects.

A business plan is essential, but it doesn't have to be documented unless more than one person is involved.

Important Engagement

A seismic data processing job was particularly satisfying to Ray because it was a refreshing change from his publishing work, involved research and travel, used his math expertise, and satisfied his client and saved them money.

The client was an engineering company based in India which wanted to explore the feasibility of, and possible methods for, creating a new seismic data processing system which could be used in oil exploration activities. Ray was invited to undertake this research because he was known to the client firm, having done business with them some years earlier. Ray spent about a year studying the issues, going to trade and technical gatherings, to the library, and meeting with technicians. His client did not want others to know of their interest in this matter, so Ray's role was something like that of a sleuth, creating an element of intrigue and excitement.

The project's conclusion was that the oil companies had developed sophisticated systems with their extensive research resources, and those systems were proprietary and closely guarded for competitive reasons. Therefore, the development of a comparable new system was determined to be financially impractical.

If the client company had not had Ray conduct this analysis, it might have launched an extensive development effort that would have been a waste of time and money. So the project paid for itself many times over.

■ ■ ■ ■

The Bassett Consulting Group, Inc.

Profile—Larry Bassett

The Bassett Consulting Group, Inc. is comprised of Lawrence C. Bassett, CMC, and a network of peers who assist him periodically when he needs to share ideas or gain a fresh perspective. Larry's consulting career has progressed through three phases, each about ten years. Phase one was with a large human resources consulting firm, phase two with a small company he founded with several associates, and the current phase is as a solo independent working out of an office attached to his home.

The present phase has been the most profitable, the most enjoyable, and has included the most challenging, interesting, and top-level engagements, though it would not have been possible without the first two phases. His earlier years included projects in human relations programs, such as labor relations, job evaluation, performance appraisal, opinion surveys, training, salaries and incentives, and suggestion plans. The more recent engagements include his broad range of regular assignments plus chief executive assessments and coaching, guidance to boards of directors, organization planning, team building, guiding reengineering programs, and an occasional executive search, which he does on special request for close clients only. He also has become a sought-after speaker.

Guiding Principles

During our interview, Larry was continually bubbling over with ideas about what it takes to be a successful independent consultant. These thoughts reveal innovative insights gleaned from his years of practice and study of people. These concepts are summarized next.

Consulting is more an art than a business. As with sales, you can't just learn some rules then follow them and be a star. It requires creativity, intuition, ingenuity. You have to have a feel for it, and do it with persistence and enthusiasm, to do it well.

Motivation is an essential ingredient in independent consulting. Feeling an intense need to achieve goals produces the determination, and sometimes that needed second wind, to stay the course and accomplish your goals.

Consultants must continuously keep up with changing technology and conditions in their fields. What was "industrial engineering" in the early 1900s to pioneers like Frederick Taylor, who some believe was the first true management consultant, and Frank Gilbreth, is now "re-engineering." Current approaches are much changed. Larry spends a lot of time reading executive book summaries and digests to stay on top of what's happening in the business world without the ponderous task of trying to get through every business book.

To become a successful independent consultant, sometimes it's easiest to start with a consulting firm to get the feel of it and develop contacts who can be useful when you are on your own. Repeat business and referrals are a consultant's most cost effective marketing strategy.

Larry finds the major benefit of being an independent consultant is the sense of control. Sure, he says, consulting is unpredictable—no assurances, no guarantees. He may not always get the engagement he seeks. But essentially he has control over his day-to-day routine. He alone, no one else, directs his activities, though each assignment has its own parameters and requirements. And the feeling of control takes the anxiety out of the normal stress from the uncertainties. There is no stress from the whims of a boss or a company policy.

When clients have a perplexing and seemingly unsolvable business problem and you enable them to set it right, "they love you forever." And Larry believes a consultant's success is in direct relation to the ability to remove frustration and anxiety from a client through effective and rapid problem solving. (When doing a job, keep in mind the client's potential for repeat business and referrals.)

Larry finds that people who persist, who rely on their native stick-to-it-ive problem-solving ability and do proper research, will get better results than more knowledgeable people who are hesitant to take on problems of uncertain dimensions or who lack self-confidence. He cited an example of a client who, after 40 years in business, was considered a walking encyclopedia in his field, but who was overjoyed with a program Larry designed for him. The client alone just couldn't put all of the pieces together. He then considered Larry an expert in a specialty in which Larry had little previous experience but in which he did careful research. The client subsequently asked Larry to provide him with further assistance "to teach him some new tricks."

Larry believes strongly that a successful consultant must understand the client's value system, biases, and idiosyncracies. Recommendations must be framed within the client's universe to be accepted. An example was a client whose business style was to have meetings to make nearly every decision. This unalterable habit was a tremendous drain on the organization's time. Larry didn't waste effort (or risk losing the client) by futilely urging the client to reduce the number of meetings. Instead, he won much gratitude by showing how meetings could be shorter, more effective, and less inconvenient.

Larry's marketing philosophy is to find out what people want and give it to them. Find out what they dislike, and avoid it. A simplistic, but worthy guideline. He asks his clients how they will measure the success of a project. He asks them to describe what they expect to happen and what end results they want. You should first find out what the client expects, then do your best to fulfill that expectation.

Larry goes a step further. "The secret of my success," Larry says, is that "I do what's necessary to give clients a little more than they expect." "I give away information, know-how, and expertise, but because a client cannot learn everything in a day, my sharing comes home as a request for more help. I call it the 'boomerang effect,'" he says. For example, Larry may take some extra time to train a client's employees in his methods so they can continue better without him. Or he may counsel a client, without charge, on a matter not related to the assignment. Those efforts pay off in referrals and in being called back more often. "By giving them more than they expected, I build a bond, a relationship."

Being laid back can often be better than being assertive. A client may feel threatened by an over-aggressive person. In his first year as a consultant, Larry accompanied a senior consultant in making a proposal. The senior consultant was a big person, with a booming voice, a real presence. He'd written books. He was "famous." In the presentation, Larry made a few remarks only to avoid being seen as too passive. But when the response came in, the client wanted Larry to do the job, not the so-called guru. Larry's temperament had the right chemistry, a manner that did not threaten the client. On the other hand, when a really secure client reacts better to a forceful presenter, Larry adopts that style.

Larry has never had a brochure, or a document describing his firm's credentials. He has not needed one, though he promotes his certification by the Institute of Management Consultants, which requires a set of high standards and ethics, and he has a one-page summary of services. His marketing has been indirect, generating inquiries and referrals from the visibility he has achieved through his teaching, seminars, extensive public speaking, a videotape about how to achieve goals, articles, a book, as well as professional association activities.

When completing an assignment, recommendations should be specific, not general. Provide details of the actions needed to correct a problem. In analyzing a person's golf swing, a coach doesn't say, "You have a bad slice and ought to do something about it." A good coach explains the specific actions that will overcome the slice. So, after conducting an opinion survey, Larry will zero in on specific actions that can be rapidly implemented. "Clients don't want to know company communications are bad. They want practical solutions."

Larry's experience has convinced him that people are not afraid of change. They are afraid of the consequences, discomfort, and impact of change—what changes may do to them. Remembering and addressing this fear can help in the design of approaches that will lessen the client's opposition to innovations.

Career Steps

Before getting into consulting, Larry held a variety of jobs, each one of which contributed to the experience and skills he later applied as a human resources consultant. His first job was at a leading Fifth Avenue retail store as a section manager and assistant buyer, learning to supervise a large staff of sales people, some of whom were old enough to be his grandmother. This experience gave him insights that still serve him 40 years later. Next Larry did a five-year stint with a freight forwarding company doing personnel work but, having little supervision, he acted as a kind of internal consultant. Then two years with a manufacturing company gave Larry some perspective on factory life, hands-on labor negotiations experience, and an awareness of the feelings and attitudes of blue-collar workers. Finally, he worked first in human resources and then as assistant hospital director with two major hospitals.

Before starting his business career, Larry served in the army at the end of the Korean War on recruiting duty, doing psychological testing. He had previously received his B.A. from New York University majoring in psychology, and subsequently received a (post-army) MBA by going to school nights at NYU while working at his day jobs.

Larry had always wanted to be a consultant. But, now married with a first child, and having finished his master's, he decided to accept the security of a "regular" job. He went to work as director of personnel at a hospital, and he was subsequently promoted to assistant director of the hospital. While there, a recruiter he knew told him of an opening with Organization Resources Counselors (ORC), a large and well-respected human resources consulting firm. Although the chair of the hospital board wanted him to stay, Larry made the break; he stayed with ORC for close to ten years, getting experience in the full range of human resources activities.

He left ORC to form a small human resources firm with two other associates. Applied Leadership Technologies, Inc. specialized in human relations consulting, offering a broad range of human resources services including advising and counseling senior management in leadership concepts and methods. The staff of ALT grew to six professionals during the ten years Larry was with the firm when the changing interests of the principals led them to break into a network of individual practitioners. Since the spring of 1986, Larry has been an independent consulting practitioner, continuing engagements from contacts developed over more than two decades with other organizations through his teaching, speaking, writing, and professional association activities. The following are a few examples of his wide variety of consulting projects:

> A sizable family-owned business which had grown rapidly recognized that it was in disarray and moving in all directions without a clear purpose. They asked Larry to help overcome the chaos and give the company an organization and direction. In one year he helped turn management from a group who were at each others' throats into a highly motivated management team working together toward well-defined and understood goals, working within a positive corporate culture.

> A large temporary office service company wanted to increase its sales. Larry accomplished that goal for them by instituting innovative techniques. One simple but powerful motivational technique was to post a graph of hours billed compared with the previous year. Based on Larry's knowledge of workers' sense of challenge, the approach resulted in an increased motivation to achieve dramatically improved billings and revenue. The client was amazed by the rapid and effective results.

Three brothers, the oldest of whom was in his mid-thirties, were running a nearly $100 million company and recognized their lack of management expertise and formal schooling. Larry gave them coaching, training, and guidance. He observed their work habits and encouraged the development of their talents by suggesting management concepts which fit into their personal styles. As a consequence the company is growing more rapidly and profitably.

He has been engaged to work with a closed board of directors. Through role playing, Larry has made them aware of the benefits of outside directors—showing how an outside director can be to their advantage and profit.

Some of Larry's consulting engagements have enabled his clients to achieve measurable beneficial results. These are representative highlights:

- Created a bonus incentive program which increased a hospital's revenues $3.5 million in three years, on a return on $292,000 in management bonuses.

- Saved $120,000 a year by suggesting the reuse of corrugated boxes for a manufacturer's warehouse operation.

- Conducted quality circle sessions to improve the effectiveness of plastic bag production. The 125 employee work force was reduced by 10 percent while production rose. And the excess workers were transferred to other departments.

- Established a quality assurance program that reduced rejects 30 percent for a Fortune 500 manufacturer.

- Persuaded a sales staff to increase productivity from 20 percent to 60 percent by training them to be persistent—to not give up when potential customers said "no."

- Counseled a hotel's managers in creative thinking. They then increased revenue and cut costs $500,000, preventing layoffs planned to resolve a cash crisis.

- Saved $250,000 a year for a hospital by working with them to establish their own blood bank rather than buying blood.

- Cut an intolerable turnover rate by 25 percent and absenteeism to near zero, in four months, by correcting problems uncovered in an opinion survey.

- Significantly reduced the average waiting time for a bank's customers to under a minute through a customer service training program.

During all his consulting career, Larry has relied on teaching, speaking, and writing as sources of modest extra income and, more importantly, as ways of enhancing his professional reputation. Larry has found that he can't expect consulting prospects always to result directly from writing and speaking, but such activities have a positive impact on his image and recognition enhancement. "If someone has heard of you often enough, read your writing, or seen your video, you are seen as an authority and then it is easier to get an assignment." He says, "There is a cumulative effect, based on the marketing principle of 'repetitive visibility.' "

He has taught management and human resources courses since 1962. He taught at Fairleigh Dickenson University for 22 years, has been an assistant professor at New York University for many years, and continues to teach graduate-level management courses at New York Medical College. He has been a guest lecturer at other universities, both here and abroad. Larry regularly gives presentations to a great variety of groups including professional associations, business groups, and corporate gatherings in addition to his client training. And, he has been a arbitrator since 1965.

His major writing was *Achieving Excellence, a Prescription for Health Care Managements*, published by Aspen Publications in 1986. Fifteen thousand copies have been sold. The substance of the book came from material Larry developed for his training courses. Larry has prepared a number of audiotapes and has a videocassette available for sale, *How You Can Achieve What Others Only Dream* and an audiocassette album, *How to Get a Good Job During Tough Times*. He's also had many articles published in professional journals and business periodicals and is acting on a personal strategic plan to produce additional videos and management books.

Demonstrating how speaking, writing, and consulting can reinforce each other, he cited an example of a $50,000 consulting job he got which would not have come his way were it not for one of the audiotapes he produced.

Larry has found that being active in professional associations has been beneficial in many ways. First, it is essential to staying on top technically, in keeping knowledgeable about the latest trends and methodologies. It can be a source of referrals—getting acquainted with people who respect you and may pass along a comment that leads to a client. And association membership reinforces a consultant's necessary image as an expert in the field. Larry keeps active with these associations: American

Society of Training and Development; National Speakers Association; Society for Human Resources Management; and Institute of Management Consultants.

Points to Remember

Consulting is more an art than a business. So follow your intuition and instincts, have confidence in them, and pursue your goals with persistence and determination.

Keep up to date with the technology and business conditions in your field and your clients' industries.

There are benefits to being with a consulting firm before launching out on your own as a solo independent.

Enjoy the benefits of being in control of your own life and activities. Let uncertainties drive you into action, not anxiety.

You are bound to succeed if you find out what people want and give it to them. Find out your clients' values and biases, and make recommendations that they are comfortable accepting.

Give everyone you meet, especially clients, a little more than they expect.

Important Engagement

An association of retail sports and ski shops retained Larry to conduct training for the shop owners. The individual stores, hundreds of them, were mostly family owned. These people knew everything about the products they sold, about skiing and other sports, and particularly about retailing. But they were interested in seeing if there really was more to learn.

Larry coached these store owners and their employees in leadership principles and methods, especially the handling of employees and how to motivate them. Using creative thinking he also taught them things about retailing and selling "they hadn't thought of." The beneficial results of this engagement were indicated by one observation by a store owner. He said to Larry, "I'm not sure what you do or how you do it, but I've been watching an employee, and I see no difference in how he is talking to people or how he is selling. All I know is that his sales have gone up 20 percent."

■ ■ ■ ■

FSL Human Resource Services

Profile—Fredrica S. Levinson

FSL Human Resource Services is the firm name of Fredrica S. Levinson. Her outstanding skills are directed at improving employee performance and results, overcoming employee productivity problems, and helping employees develop their strengths through training and counseling. Her education, experience, and innate analytical talent enable her to determine issues that lie behind the symptoms of a problem and develop corrective measures as well as other improvements. She does this by conducting needs assessments, evaluating work situations and people's behavior, then designing training programs and making recommendations for actions to accomplish her clients' desired goals. Her many top-level clients have been delighted with the results she has helped them achieve in sales, customer service, productivity, quality, and morale. Many clients call her back to tackle new issues.

Guiding Principles

Fredrica got started in consulting almost by accident, by being asked by an organization to address a broad range of productivity problems in another country over a period of several years. When that experience convinced her that consulting was the path for her, she embarked on a vigorous marketing promotion at a trade show which resulted in being requested to make a presentation at a national trade association. The presentation, in turn, produced contacts for two new engagements. From then on, she kept continually busy by "keeping her name out there" via talks, participation in professional and business groups, interviews on radio and TV, and ads in the yellow pages. Her marketing scheme is "networking, networking, networking." Twice when long and heavy engagements prevented networking, slow consulting periods followed. This was quickly rectified by resuming her strong but indirect marketing approach.

A major feature of her operating philosophy is to analyze problems in depth and tailor make solutions to real needs. She abhors the idea of "canned" training or pep talks to improve motivation. She finds that the real needs are often quite different from what the clients have perceived them to be. Her solutions, therefore, require diplomacy, explanations, and selling to the decision-makers before the remedial actions are carried out. And her solutions are always based on in-depth needs analyses conducted through interviews, on-the-job observations, surveys, or whatever is required. Her training programs are participative and lively and usually include exercises, case studies, role playing, and much discussion.

Career Steps Fredrica's education includes a B.S. in education from the State University of New York at Potsdam, an M.A. in counseling from New York University, management science courses at George Washington University's School of Engineering and Applied Science, and study with the leading authority on quality improvement, Dr. W. Edwards Deming.

Her human relations skills were honed at Federation Employment and Guidance Service (New York), beginning as a counselor and ending up—five years and three promotions later—in charge of over 25 staff members including counselors, teachers, and evaluators at the FEGS's Manhattan Diagnostic Vocational Evaluation facility in the United States. This organization evaluated approximately two thousand persons a year, people with physical and emotional disabilities, substance abuse problems, developmental disabilities, and antisocial behavior. Through skills and work behavior analysis, training, and guidance FEGS helped these individuals change their work behaviors and attitudes so that they could become useful and self-respecting individuals and learn specific job skills.

Next came a three-year stint as Director of Career Counseling at Sarah Lawrence College, continuing her professional experience in dealing with the relationships of people to their work.

Then in 1981 she started a Ph.D. program in industrial/organizational psychology at Rutgers University. Several things happened at about that time which turned her career toward consulting. She dropped the Rutgers program because of her children and family needs. She also had become heavily involved in a wide range of community work in her field, such as conducting workshops and making presentations on mental health matters and vocational issues for women.

One of her contacts asked her to give a series of seminars at a growing enterprise, an artists' village in the Dominican Republic. What they really needed was management development. Fredrica was asked back four or five times a year for several years to help advise, train, and guide them as they developed their expanding tourist and cultural businesses projects. It was interesting. There were new hotels, restaurants, boutiques, art galleries, museums, a 5,000-seat amphitheater, and people from the U.S., Latin America, and Europe. She found she particularly enjoyed the role of freelance trainer and presenter. Her five years as a teacher and her group and individual work as a counselor helped make it easy to facilitate groups and guide individuals. She found she gained a great deal of satisfaction from evaluating work situations and people's behavior, analyzing what they needed, and designing programs to help people meet their goals.

During this Dominican Republic period, Fredrica was also involved in a variety of activities such as coordinating education services at the Intrepid Sea-Air Space Museum and serving as a counselor and presenter for community groups.

Having become a successful consultant without consciously planning to become one, and enjoying it, Fredrica decided to make consulting her career direction. So she launched a marketing effort by having brochures made up, with a logo and all, and preparing an exhibit at a trade show sponsored by the New Jersey Business and Industry Association. This created a professional identity, with a focus on employee productivity improvement, which she liked doing and was good at.

One contact from that trade show asked her to make a presentation on Retention and Motivation of Middle Managers in Retail, to a group of retail executives. After that presentation, three people approached her, one just to "pick her brains," but the other two contacts ended up developing into consulting engagements for two well-known retail firms. So then she was off and running as a consultant. She moved into an office of sublet space. While she recognizes that working from home is quite feasible for many consultants, for her the separation of domestic and vocational venues is important. She likes the contacts with others in the office area, and she feels more comfortable in a place that is designed for business only.

After her early spurt of engagements, Fredrica learned that there can be no relaxing of the marketing effort. The lead time between making contacts and getting an assignment can be long and, at best, is of uncertain duration. Therefore, it is essential to continue "networking, networking, networking" while engagements are underway. Keeping the contacts warm and growing in number requires scheduling time each month and week. In her case, being available to give professional talks is an important element, as she likes working with groups of people, and training, like teaching and group counseling, requires group facilitation.

But Fredrica also makes a point of joining professional organizations, such as the Institute of Industrial Engineers, the Institute of Management Consultants, the American Society for Training and Development, and the American Counseling Association, and business groups such as Rotary and her local Chamber of Commerce.

Taking on committee work and officer positions in these groups, as well as speaking before them, has resulted in requests to undertake consulting and training. The professional associations have also, of course, helped her to keep abreast of current developments in her specialization.

The other way she has found to keep in the public's eye as a professional has been offering to be interviewed on TV and radio programs and being profiled in periodicals. Many of her media interviews have been on sexual harassment issues on which she has performed some consulting engagements.

In 1989, Fredrica decided to put her consulting business on hold because the time demands of consulting did not jibe with the demands of her personal life. She responded to an ad for Manager of Customer Service and Training at a Bloomingdale's store. She easily got the job because the person who placed the ad was someone Fredrica had interviewed while researching a presentation, someone who was already aware of Fredrica's talents. Fredrica stayed there for a year-and-a-half and then reestablished her consulting business, setting up an office first in Jamaica, Long Island, and then moving the office to Forest Hills. To regain her consulting momentum, she launched several new networking activities including joining Rotary and the Chamber of Commerce, and she also placed a few one-inch ads in the business-to-business yellow pages.

To give you a flavor of her approach and the results she has accomplished for her clients, the following are capsules of some of her engagements.

A company wanted a total quality improvement program. FSL trained over 600 employees, covering new procedures to benefit customers. Thereafter, customer compliments increased threefold, and complaints decreased over 50 percent. The client continued to call on FSL for follow-up training and guidance.

A client asked FSL to evaluate an executive whose performance was poor. FSL found the executive was in the wrong job, recommended she head a new joint venture being started. The proposed change was made, the venture became a success, and the client's senior management was extremely pleased.

Another client's general manager, promoted there after a 20-year climb, was unduly stressed, worked 60-hour weeks, underperforming. After extensive coaching and training by FSL in such skills as delegation, communication, team development, and time management, the manager became completely comfortable and effective in that role.

A telemarketing company was losing sales. FSL developed better telemarketing approaches and methods after conducting needs analysis discussions with top management and telemarketing employees and on-the- job observation. After training telemarketers in the new and better ways, the company's slide in sales was reversed.

A mid-sized company with over a thousand sales calls a week was losing potential business. FSL was asked to improve its customer service and sales department. That department's staff lacked motivation and knowledge of techniques for pleasing customers. After sales training sessions, they sold more products and increased premium sales by listening to customers' needs and showing interest in them. The sales staff's self-esteem and enthusiasm rose. Product sales increased 20 percent over the prior period.

A transportation services company requested a training program for its 80 customer service employees. After that was done, the client was very satisfied with the training results and called FSL back to conduct training for the accounts payable people handling their collection calls.

While most of FSL's clients have been medium-sized firms, its client list does include some well-known organizations such as Aetna, Fordham University, General Motors, NBO Stores, New York City's Mayor's Office, and The Prudential Insurance Company of America.

Points to Remember Fredrica Levinson's experience and ideas illustrate a number of key points.

While Fredrica got started in consulting by being asked and without any marketing effort at all, once she got started she could keep up the momentum only by continually using a great variety of efforts to "get your name out there," and "networking, networking, networking."

Her talent and demand as a speaker are her primary means for becoming known and respected and making contacts. But she also is active in many professional and business organizations, and has been asked to be interviewed in the media on topics in her field.

She points out that being an independent consultant can be like a roller coaster. You must be comfortable with this somewhat iffy business to succeed in it. Continuous networking is the best means Fredrica has found to keep the business moving along.

Another observation she has made is that much consulting is crisis driven. Many, if not most, consulting engagements arise when a client is confronted with some unexpected condition and then wants or needs urgent help. So it behooves a consultant to be prepared and flexible, ready to jump in to diagnose and help resolve a problem when requested.

Important Engagement

One engagement was particularly satisfying for Fredrica because her skills and approach were well suited to help resolve a problem the client had recognized but had been unable to deal with. The results pleased both the client and consultant, and led to follow-up assignments on unrelated problems that Fredrica helped resolve easily and well.

A large food company contacted Fredrica, at the suggestion of someone else, because they were dissatisfied with the results their service representatives were achieving but were unable to pinpoint why. The client thought maybe these reps were incompetent, and maybe they should fire and replace them. In analyzing the situation, Fredrica interviewed the representatives and found them to be untrained. They didn't know proper methods for dealing with customers, didn't have product knowledge, and hadn't even seen the products. But they were not stupid; they had the requisite potential ability.

So Fredrica designed and conducted a training program to correct these deficiencies. She got them familiar with their products. She taught them sales techniques and the methods for dealing effectively with their customers. The results were that customer turnover dropped dramatically and sales increased. The client and the newly trained reps were all happy.

A few months later the client called Fredrica again to resolve problems with two new managers. They were both motivated and talented but neither had any experience before as a manager. Secondly, they were at odds with each other. Fredrica conducted an intensive training program for them in management skills. And, as an experienced counselor, worked with the two of them to turn the adversarial relationship into a harmonious one.

Some months later the client again called on her, this time to help train a person who had been with the company 12 years, had been promoted to manager, was talented and bright, but did not have managerial skills. Fredrica took her on and gave her one-on-one training and counseling in the art of managing, creating the capability the manager needed.

■ ■ ■ ■

Williams, Brown & Co., Inc
Profile—Carol Brown

Williams, Brown & Co., Inc. consists of Carol W. Brown and three assistants; two are employees, and one is a subcontractor. Williams is Carol's maiden name, Brown her married name. Carol Brown, the founder and prime mover of the firm, has found and filled a unique customer niche, computer systems for distinguished clubs in New York City. She has become successful in that field because of her talent for and persistence in becoming a top-notch hands-on programmer, her determination to listen to what the clients say is needed and to fulfill those needs, and her passion for making operations simple and easy.

Guiding Principles

Carol Brown has strong feelings about how to deal with clients and her own staff.

With clients, she says they know what they want and need, and it is essential to listen to them. She has developed long-term and continuing relationships with her clients, and that would not be possible without achieving a feeling of trust and a reputation for complete honesty. While the original engagements were based on written proposals, day-to-day work is requested orally, without question; clients know that her bill will be fair and reasonable. She has often helped them out of a jam in matters beyond her computer consulting responsibility, and her clients have expressed their appreciation for that.

She also endeavors to form a relationship of respect and trust, and of genuine friendliness, with her staff members. Each knows how the others work, and support for each other predominates rather than competition. "Cooperation" she says "is the grease that makes the wheels go round."

Career Steps

Carol started her career as a management trainee at the Metropolitan Life Insurance Company's headquarters after graduating from Wellesley in 1962. At Met Life she got a lot of experience in work measurement and simplification, using a stopwatch to help develop time standards as well as better systems and methods. To achieve skills in the coming computer arena, Carol took all the courses she could on evenings and Saturdays, studying systems and programming at New York University from which she received a Certificate in Computer Programming and Systems Analysis.

Her next step was to join the premier consulting firm, McKinsey & Company, Inc., four years later. But she was not a consultant as such at McKinsey. As manager of computer systems there, her job was to design and program procedures on their new computer used for accounting and reports, as well as to manage computer and data entry operations. Her six years at McKinsey sharpened her hands-on skills for what she would later do as a consultant: design and program management and financial systems for her clients.

Realizing that, at that time, leadership positions at firms like McKinsey were held almost exclusively by men, she thought she'd try to apply her skills as a freelance consultant. She got her first independent engagement developing a computerized accounting system for a magazine publisher. That worked fine, except that in the first month the general ledger didn't balance. She realized that her accounting knowledge was inadequate, and quickly rectified that by correcting the design after checking out the accounting principles involved. Her openness with the client about acknowledging the problem and rectifying it made the client happy with her and the final results.

Her next major engagement was with an architectural firm and lasted for 15 years. This job resulted from an introduction by the architect husband of a friend of hers. That firm had an early computer-assisted-design system. She designed and implemented the firm's computer accounting procedures, integrated them with the design and operations systems, and developed an office-planning system for forecasting their clients' future personnel, equipment, and space needs.

In 1983, four years after starting with the architects, Carol was retained by one of the largest college clubs in New York City to establish and computerize its membership record keeping and accounting. The club's accounting firm had written the system's goals and specs, and she made a proposal for designing and implementing programs to achieve those goals. The lead, again, was a referral through a friend.

That first club job became the basis for the main thrust of her consulting in the years ahead, with clubs in New York City as clients. Her success and reputation for designing and implementing effective computer systems led to subsequent engagements at three other Ivy League college clubs, and the renowned restaurant, The 21 Club. All of these engagements are continuing as of this writing. These engagements have similar requirements: tracking their member/customer base, restaurant and bar sales, banquet business, and hotel-like room services. Some clubs also provide athletic facilities.

Because of these similarities in the organizations Carol serves, a system innovation developed for one of them can often be adapted to others. There is no conflict between clients because these organizations really do not compete. Many staff members have been with other clubs and their attitude has always been friendly toward the others. At the same time, Carol maintains that a cookie-cutter approach cannot be applied; each organization's needs are different and the systems and programs must be tailor-made to fit their individual requirements.

The extra efforts Carol expends and innovative simplifications she puts into club systems explain her strong reputation and steady flow of clients. For example, when some billing errors caused by incorrect source data came to light, which had obviously annoyed members, she designed controls which automatically prevented most of those errors. When a group of billings were lost because of an unaccountable slipup, Carol pitched in to identify which were lost and recreated them, even though it was not her responsibility. When she saw people making 800 billing entries for 800 members who attended a New Year's Eve party, she devised a method for entering them as a group rather than individually, a simplified method which was subsequently applied to many other group charges, like the billings for lockers. When she discovered that monthly statements were handled differently because of different postage, delinquency letters, and other needs, she instituted sorts by such groups to simplify handling them. The club's controller told her he was impressed by how far she would go to make their processes easier and simpler.

While each of the club engagements began with a carefully written contract of what was to be done, when, and at what cost, her continuing work has usually become informally arranged. She and the client discuss current needs, the client says go ahead, and Carol bills on a time basis with few questions asked. Part of her continuing work is based on need changes, new activities to computerize, refinements, and her philosophy that she wants to be a major part of implementation of all the systems she designs and programs. For example, some clubs are instituting minimum charges for members, which require a whole new set of record-keeping processes. Carol is not satisfied unless she is there to make sure everything works, and works well.

Carol insists on modems at each client's site to simplify and expedite her work. She can dial in to make adjustments from another client's office or from her home to accomplish a needed change quickly. Also, she wrote many lines of code at home during the months she was taking care of her small baby.

Incidentally, Carol holds the copyrights to the programs she has designed, but her contracts give her clients permanent license to use them.

The club programs Carol Brown has designed mostly have been done with minicomputers using the Pick operating system. That operating system is an excellent and older system which, while very efficient, never became very popular. As the Windows operating system is becoming almost a universal standard, many of her clients may well want to convert to Windows, partly because many prospective employees may be already familiar with it. If so, that may make for a substantial phase of further refinements and continuing engagements with the same clients.

During her consulting career, Carol has written and lectured extensively on computer subjects. In the 1980s she wrote *The Minicomputer Simplified: An Executive's Guide to the Basics* and chapters in two computer handbooks, all published by Macmillan Publishing Co., Inc. And she led panel groups and lectured at conferences for groups such as the National Computer Conference and the Data Processing Management Association. She has also been active in the Association of Computing Machinery.

Points to Remember   Much of the success of the Williams, Brown Co., Inc. can be attributed to these philosophies and activities of Carol Brown:

> Find a special need, specialty, or niche and become the most knowledgeable person to serve that area.
>
> Do a little extra for your clients, more than they bargained for.

Be completely honest and above-board in dealing with your clients, and make sure they know that.

Don't oversell your capability. If you do make that mistake inadvertently, acknowledge it, and correct it on your own time and at your own expense.

A consulting firm can grow into a gradually expanding business without any special marketing campaign, by developing a reputation early on, and through referrals from normal business and personal contacts.

Carol Brown never found a need for a written plan. She just started off on the first engagement and grew as opportunities presented themselves.

APPENDIX B: Bibliography[1]

Bellman, Geoffrey M., *The Consultant's Calling*, Jossey-Bass, 1990. This "soft" work encourages us to step back and think about what we're doing and where we're going, to put life in perspective.

Bermont, Hubert, *How to Become a Successful Consultant in Your Own Field,* 3rd edition, Bermont Books, 1992. Highly personalized account of how one solo made it, full of practical advice for beginners. First of the genre we can recommend. Very easy reading.

Brown, Peter C., *Jumping the Job Track: Security, Satisfaction, and Success as an Independent Consultant*, New York: Crown Publishers, Inc., 1994.

The Chicago Manual of Style, Chicago: The University of Chicago Press, 1993.

[1]Comments quoted from Management Consulting Books, a free catalog of Consultants Bookstore, Kennedy Publications, Fitzwilliam, New Hampshire (800–531–0007).

Connor, Richard A., Jr. and Davidson, Jeffrey P., *Getting New Clients*, Wiley, 1993. A Betty Crocker cookbook in Silver Palate times, this work still fills the need for a pedestrian/workmanlike/detailed approach to business-getting "the old fashioned way." Highly recommended for beginners and smaller firms who've never taken the time to do the kind of market research they should have, or need to reorient a sick or plateaued practice.

Consulting & Consulting Organizations Directory, 15th edition, Detroit, MI: Gale Research Inc., 1994.

The Directory of Executive Temporary Placement Firms, Fitzwilliam, NH: Kennedy Publications, 1995.

The Directory of Management Consultants, 1995–1996, Kennedy Publications, Fitzwilliam, NH. Profiles of 1,500 management consulting firms. Paragraph description followed by billings and staff-size ranges, with four indexes: services offered, industries served, geographic and key principals. Information on consulting associations with frank advice on selecting consultants.

Edwards, Paul and Sarah, and Douglas, Laura Clampitt, *Getting Business to Come to You*, Los Angeles: Jeremy P. Tarcher, Inc., 1991.

Edwards, Paul and Sarah, *Making It on Your Own, Surviving and Thriving on the Ups and Downs of Being Your Own Boss*, Los Angeles: Jeremy P. Tarcher, Inc., 1991.

Edwards, Paul and Sara, *Working from Home, Everything You Need to Know about Living and Working under the Same Roof*, New York: G. P. Putnam's Sons, 1994.

Holtz, Herman, *The Business Plan Guide for Independent Consultants*, New York: John Wiley & Sons, Inc., 1994.

Holtz, Herman, *Computer Consulting on Your Home-Based PC*, New York: Windcrest/McGraw-Hill, 1994.

Holtz, Herman, *How to Succeed as an Independent Consultant*, 3d ed., New York: John Wiley & Sons, Inc., 1993.

Huang, Kelly, editor, *Management Consulting 1995*, Boston: Harvard Business School Press, 1995.

Kamoroff, Bernard, *Small-Time Operator—How to Start Your Own Small Business, Keep Your Books, Pay Your Taxes, and Stay Out of Trouble!*, Laytonville, CA: Bell Springs Publishing, 1992.

Lant, Jeffrey L., *The Consultant's Kit: Establishing and Operating Your Successful Consulting Business*, JLA Publications, 1991. Lots of helpful information for neophytes in breezy gee-whiz style. Includes sample sales letters, proposals, contracts.

Lewin, Marsha D., *The Overnight Consultant*, New York: John Wiley & Sons, Inc., 1995.

Literary Market Place, New Providence, NJ: R. R. Bowker, 1995.

Marcus, Bruce W., *Competing for Clients in the 90s*, Provus, 1992. Recognizes every firm's need for a planned and coordinated marketing effort to survive and grow these days. A veritable A-B-C, how-to-do- it— from the mind-set to execution. Shows how what's been done in accounting and law applies to consulting as well. A valuable reference that will become dog-eared.

Marketing and Matchmaking for Management Consultants, Fitzwilliam, NH: Kennedy Publications, 1995.

Metzger, Robert O., *Developing a Consulting Practice*, Sage, 1993. Aptly emphasizing its importance, marketing dominates the first half of this little book. Written primarily for professors in all disciplines who want to consult but of benefit to all neophyte wannabe consultants.

Quay, John, *Diagnostic Interviewing for Consultants and Auditors*, Quay, 1994. Even old salts can fine-tune interviewing techniques with this helpful guide! Tells how to chart and control interviews to extract maximum information painlessly, including five "softening" hints when probing sensitive areas.

Service Annual Survey: 1993, BS/93, U.S. Department of Commerce, Economics and Statistics Administration, Bureau of the Census.

Shenson, Howard L., *Shenson on Consulting*, Wiley, 1990. More aptly titled *Sales and Marketing Basics for the Solo Consultant*, this fine roundup belongs in every beginner's library. Conveniently packaged in 97 bite-sized segments.

Simon, Alan R., *How to Be a Successful Computer Consultant*, New York: McGraw-Hill, Inc., 1994.

Tepper, Ron, *Become a Top Consultant—How the Experts Do It*, New York: John Wiley & Sons, 1985.

Thomsett, Michael C., *The Consultant's Money Book*, Bermont books, 1987. A simple and direct explanation of the consultant's needs in an accounting system: record-keeping, financial statements, basic controls, ratios.

Weiss, Alan, *Million Dollar Consulting, The Professional's Guide to Growing a Practice*, New York: McGraw-Hill, 1992. This book will jolt you out of conventional approaches to building a consulting business. Cycling from the profound to the mundane, and written in a brash braggadocial style, the book alternately challenges and bores. Whether you agree with his ideas or not, defending your position will help you clarify your own game plan ... solid underlining of ethical practice on such topics as referral and contingent fees, reimbursed expenses, and true client service.

1992 Census of Service Industries, SC92–A–52, Geographic Area Series, United States, U.S. Department of Commerce, Economics and Statistics Administration, Bureau of the Census.